# THE *Fly Fishing* ANTHOLOGY

Voyageur Press

Compiled and edited by Danielle J. Ibister
Designed by Maria A. Friedrich
Printed in China

04 05 06 07 08 5 4 3 2 1

Library of Congress Cataloging-in-Publication Data

The fly fishing anthology / compiled and edited by Danielle J. Ibister.
p. cm.
ISBN 0-89658-655-3 (hardcover)
1. Fly fishing. I. Ibister, Danielle J.
SH456.F5852 2004
799.12'4—dc22
2004002637

Distributed in Canada by Raincoast Books
9050 Shaughnessy Street
Vancouver, B.C. V6P 6E5

Published by Voyageur Press, Inc.
123 North Second Street, P.O. Box 338
Stillwater, MN 55082 U.S.A.
651-430-2210, fax 651-430-2211
books@voyageurpress.com
www.voyageurpress.com



FRONT COVER PHOTO CREDITS:
LEFT INSET AND BACKGROUND IMAGE:
*Photographs © R. Valentine Atkinson*
MIDDLE AND RIGHT INSETS:
*Photographs © Doug Stamm*

PAGE 1: *This still life showcases a Vom Hoff fly reel. (Photograph © Howard Lambert)*

PAGE 2: *Rushing water surrounds an angler fishing Big Springs, a glacier-fed spring that flows into California's McCloud River. (Photograph © R. Valentine Atkinson)*

PAGE 3: *A Montana fisherman reaches for his catch in the Gardiner River. (Courtesy of the Montana Historical Society, Helena)*

PAGE 4: *Sunset finds a fly fisherman throwing the final cast on the Snake River. (Photograph © R. Valentine Atkinson)*

PAGE 6: *A fly line swirls over the head of an angler fishing DePuy's Spring Creek. (Photograph © R. Valentine Atkinson)*

# Contents

CHAPTER ONE

# To Make a Fly Fisherman

"I BEGAN TO NOTICE THE GRACE INVOLVED IN A SIMPLE CAST, HOW THE ARM OF A GOOD ANGLER WAS MERELY AN EXTENSION OF THE FLY ROD."

*–Lorian Hemingway, "Walk on Water for Me"*

# *Fly Fishing Through the Midlife Crisis*

*By Howell Raines*

Howell Hiram Raines made an exceptional contribution to the world of fly fishing literature with the publication of his 1993 memoir, *Fly Fishing Through the Midlife Crisis.* Ripe with humor and insight, this book examines a life journey from ignorance to enlightenment—all from the perspective of a trout fisherman.

Known as the fallen executive editor of the *New York Times*, Raines is first and foremost a stellar writer. A Southerner, Raines got his start as a reporter with the Birmingham *Post-Herald* in 1964. He wrote the celebrated oral history *My Soul is Rested: Movement Days in the Deep South Remembered* (1977) and won the Pulitzer Prize for his feature article "Grady's Gift" (1992).

In this excerpt from his memoir, Raines uses a sharp yet compassionate pen to describe the South of his birth and the beginnings of his philosophical journey.

PREVIOUS PAGE, MAIN IMAGE: *An angler casts across the wide expanse of the Belize flats. (Photograph © Doug Stamm)*

PREVIOUS PAGE, INSET IMAGE: *A fisherman prepares his fly for Florida's Hillsborough River in this 1958 photograph. (Courtesy of the Florida State Archives)*

LEFT: *Distant mist and sere fields lend majesty to the fishing experience at California's Hat Creek. (Photograph © R. Valentine Atkinson)*

LIKE MANY SOUTHERNERS, I was ruined for church by early exposure to preachers. So when I need to hear the sigh of the Eternal, I find myself drawn to a deep hollow between Fork Mountain and Double Top Mountain on the eastern flank of the Blue Ridge. This is where the Rapidan River plunges through a hemlock forest and through gray boulders that jut from the ferny earth like the aboriginal bones of old Virginia. This is a place of enlightenment for me, the spot where I received the blessing of my middle years. Here, after three decades of catching fish, I began learning to fish.

At this point it is necessary to introduce Mr. Richard C. Blalock, a man given to pronouncements. There are two reasons for this trait. As a former officer of the Foreign Service of the United States, he is a natural-born pontificator. Also, Dick Blalock serves as the fly-fishing guru for a handful of people around Washington, and some of us provoke his speechifying for our own enjoyment.

*A bamboo fly rod and a colorful Jock Scott fly. (Photograph © Doug Stamm)*

I'll try to give you a sample of the conversation in Dick's loose-jointed old Chevy as it grinds along the road that the Marines scraped across the mountains in 1929 so that Herbert Hoover could reach the Rapidan. In those days, the stream was reserved for his exclusive use. President Hoover liked to fish. He also needed a place where he would not be bothered by the little people while he planned the Great Depression. I find it impossible to visit the Rapidan without a haunted feeling in regard to Herbert Hoover, but more on that later. First, the fish and the river, according to the teachings of Dick Blalock.

"This species of brook trout has never been stocked in this stream. They go back to the Ice Age. That means they have been here in this form, just as we see them today, for ten thousand years. They are survivors." That is what Dick always says to newcomers by way of inspiring respect for the Rapidan and its tenacious little genetic warriors.

"They are the most beautiful fish that God ever put on this earth. When they are in their spawning colors, they are just breathtaking," he adds for those who need prompting to adore the lush greens and pinks, the unmitigated reds of *Salvelinus fontinalis*—"the little salmon of the waterfall."

Then he enunciates Blalock's Rapidan Paradox. "These brook trout will strike any fly you present, provided you don't get close enough to present it." This means the fish are predatory, but skittish. More to the point, pursuing them prepares us to receive the central teaching of Blalock's Way. To achieve mastery is to rise above the need to catch fish.

This part did not come easily for me. I was born in the heart of Dixie and raised in the Redneck Way of Fishing, which holds that the only good trip is one ending in many dead fish. These fish might then be eaten, frozen, given to neighbors or used for fertilizer. But fishing that failed to produce an abundance of corpses could no more be successful than a football season in which the University of Alabama failed to win a national championship.

Of course, not even Bear Bryant won every year. Similarly, the greatest fishermen get skunked. So it is inevitable that the Redneck Way, which is built around the ideas of lust and conquest, will lead to failure. In that way, it resembles our physical lives. In the days of youth, when the blood is hot and the sap is high and the road goes on forever, it is easy enough to slip the doomy embrace of frustration. But time, as a British poet once said, is a rider that breaks us all, especially if our only pleasure—in football, fishing or love—comes from keeping score.

*A fisherman readies his fly at Minto Flats, an interior Alaska wetland. (Photograph © Dennis Frates)*

By the time I reached my late thirties, my passion for fishing brought with it an inexpressible burden of anxiety. As Saturday approached or, worse, a vacation, the questions would whirl through my brain. *How many* would I catch? *How big* would they be? Would my trip be *wonderful*? Would I be a *success*? I had reached the destination of all who follow the Redneck Way. I had made my hobby into work.

Then one day in the summer of 1981 I found myself at the L. L. Bean store in Freeport, Maine. I was a correspondent at the White House in those days, and my work—which consisted of reporting on President Reagan's success in making life harder for citizens who were not born rich, white and healthy—saddened me. In fact, hanging around the Reagan crowd made me yearn for connection with something noble and uplifting. I bought a fly rod.

I do not know if you are familiar with the modern fly rod, but it is one of the glories of industry. The maker starts with a toothpick of steel called a mandrel. Around this mandrel are laid miles of thread spun from graphite. The mandrel is slipped out, and this long taper is then painted with epoxy, producing a deep, mirrored finish of the sort one saw on the German automobiles of thirty years ago.

The result is a piece of magic, an elegant thing, willowy and alive—a wand that when held in the hand communicates with the heart. And the more I waved such a wand over the next few years, the more the scales of my old fish-killing heart fell away. At last I stood on the threshold of being what I had tried so hard, yet so blindly, to be since that sublime spring day in 1950 when my father and mother helped me catch twenty crappies from the Tennessee River. In the ensuing decades, I had killed hundreds of fish—bass, crappies, bluegills, shellcrackers, pike, king mackerels, red snappers, black snappers, redfish, bluefish, pompanos, amberjacks, jack crevalles, barracudas. I had been blooded in the Redneck Way by those who understood fishing as a sport and a competition. Now I was about to meet a man who understood it as an art, a pastime, a way of living easefully in the world of nature. One day my telephone rang and it was Dick Blalock.

I like to say I got my guru from the U.S. government. He was fifty-five years old when I first saw him and already a walking medical disaster. Dick played football for a season at the University of Oklahoma, but in the ensuing years he had open heart surgery and gained weight. The big event in his medical history—and his angling history, for that matter—was a liver parasite contracted in North Yemen, where he was working as a Foreign Service officer. The government pressed him to take medical retirement and a pension when he was thirty-seven.

"So I decided that if they were so determined to pay me not to work, I'd take advantage of the opportunity and go fishing for a while," Dick told me on the day we met. "That was over seventeen years ago."

"So, how's it been?" I said.

"Terrific," he said. "I'd recommend it to anyone."

As Dick Blalock spoke these words, we were rolling through northern Maryland on the enticing roads that Robert E. Lee followed to his mistake at Gettysburg. Dick had spotted an article I had written for the sports section of *The New York Times* on bass fishing in the Potomac, and he called out of the blue to say maybe it was time I tried my hand on trout. He suggested the limestone creeks of Cumberland County, Pennsylvania, holy territory for fly fishers since before the Civil War.

*Morning mist rises around an angler fishing the Yellowstone River at Nez Perce Ford. (Photograph © Jeff Henry/Roche Jaune Pictures, Inc.)*

It was a day I will not forget. At the Letort Spring Run, we watched huge brown trout fighting for spawning sites. In deference to the wishes of Charlie Fox, a venerable fly fisherman who lives near the Letort and dislikes having his trout disturbed during procreation, we did not fish. Later, on nearby Yellow Breeches Creek, I caught my first brown trout on a fly. Actually, at the time, I wasn't entirely sure whether it was a brown or a rainbow. But I guessed correctly, sparing myself embarrassment under the eyes of my new friend. Then, in accordance with the catch-and-release rules of the limestone creeks, I set the fish free. This occasioned the first Blalockian pronouncement I was to hear.

"I will never kill another trout," he said. "I release every one I catch, no matter what the regulations call for.

There are too few of them in the world, and each one is too precious to do something as wasteful as eating it."

Driving back to Washington that night, I was seized by a sneaky kind of joy, a feeling not altogether in keeping (I thought then) with the fact that I had caught only one fish—quite by accident, really—and killed none. This feeling was a clue. Soon I would be ready for the Rapidan.

Like many things in Virginia, the river was named for a member of the British royal family: Queen Anne. Being swift, it was called the Rapid Anne and, in time, the Rapidan. When we first got there in 1985, spring had come with an abrupt glory. Daffodils and forsythia bloomed on the banks, marking the homesites of the mountaineers who had been evicted by creation of the Shenandoah National Park. My sons Ben and Jeff were fifteen and thirteen. I was forty-two.

FLY FISHING.

*A woeful fly fisher surveys his handiwork in this 1879 Currier & Ives lithograph.*

We began our apprenticeships at stream fishing together. It was a painful business, learning to cast without hanging the flies in the trees, conquering the clumsiness of foot that is as much an enemy in wading as in dancing. One of the saddest sights I have ever seen was Ben returning to camp with his new Orvis rod—a Christmas trophy—shattered in a fall on slick boulders.

But in time we were skilled enough to defy Blalock's Rapidan Paradox. We learned to creep to the rim of crystal-clear pools without spooking their fish. We learned to whip our flies under limbs and drop them like live things into a living current. These matters take concentration, and the stream graded us unforgivingly. The only passing mark was a fish flashing into the visible world to strike more quickly than a finger-snap.

It is fishing I would have disdained in years past for the fragility of the tackle and the tininess of the fish. Eight inches is an average brook trout, ten a large one, anything over eleven inches a whopper. A few people, including Dick Blalock, have caught accurately measured twelve-inchers, or so they said.

Dick told us of his catch at a time when I was boasting about my liberation from the competitiveness that is part of the Redneck Way. I no longer had to catch the most fish or the biggest fish. That is what I said. In fact, Dick's twelve-inch brook trout filled me with a sudden bolt of envy.

So there came the day when Dick and I took Bill Dunlap, my friend from Mississippi, to the river. Bill is a painter with a special eye for the Virginia landscape, and I wanted him to see the shapes and colors of the Rapidan. At the time, he was in that stage of his fly-fishing novitiate in which every cast develops into an accident, so he contented himself with watching me fish one particularly sweet pool.

Straightaway, I caught my largest Rapidan trout, a deep-bellied fish that I guessed to be at least thirteen inches long. Before releasing it, I carefully marked its length on my rod, and we hurried downstream to borrow Dick's tape measure. My trophy measured eleven and one-half inches.

Later, I admired the symmetry of the experience. I had created a competition for myself and then lost it. It was yet another lesson in listening to the song of Rapid Anne. It is a song, among other things, about conquering greed and learning one's place....

This is a lesson that Henry Beston set down more than sixty years ago in a book called *The Outermost House.* "For the animals shall not be measured by man," he wrote. "They are not brethren, they are not underlings; they are other nations, caught with ourselves in the net of life and time, fellow prisoners of the splendor and travail of the earth."

To embrace this knowledge in one's inmost heart is to depart from the Redneck Way and to know, as Dick Blalock says, that "fishing is not about food." It is a way of interrupting the invisibility of these shining creatures and existing for a moment with them in their wildness and transience, their indifference to our approval and their dependence on our restraint if they are to add another hour to their ten thousandth year.

Henry Beston wrote of splendor. On the Rapidan one day I saw snow fall through blooming dogwoods. I do not expect to see such a multiplication of whiteness again in my lifetime, but it is a part of me to be lived again whenever I pull a Rapidan trout into our half of the world or, for that matter, when I contemplate these words which somehow seem to tumble together toward poetry, or song:

Rapidan.
Rapid Anne.
Rap-i-dan.
Rapidan.

*An angler displays his quarry: a healthy-sized, fly-caught rainbow trout. (Photograph © R. Valentine Atkinson)*

Throwing Slack, or Seeming Not to Care

There is a motion that is central to the Redneck Way of Fishing. I saw it demonstrated in its purest form one day in Buck's Pocket, the mountain gorge that was flooded by South Sauty Creek when Guntersville Dam was completed in 1939. The fishing at the bridge on South Sauty had played out by the mid-Fifties, but there were still plenty of big fish within reach of the outboard boat that my father kept at the South Sauty Fish Camp. Whenever someone told you he had been "back in the Pocket," you knew he had made the long run to the spot where South Sauty Creek entered the lake.

The steep mountainsides were covered with beech, hickory and oak, and wherever one of these trees had toppled into the lake, crappie were apt to gang up around the submerged treetop.

On the day I had in mind, my father and his first cousin, Hartley Best, and I were "fishing the tops" when a lanky countryman emerged from the forest. He wore overalls and carried a pole and a large tin can which, it soon became apparent, was serving as his minnow bucket. He baited up and made a whistling cast that plunked his bobber down near our boat. He set the butt of his pole in the bank, and paying us no attention, he hunkered, in true, old-time hillbilly fashion, with his feet flat on the ground, his butt on his heels and his forearms resting loosely on his knees.

Presently, his bobber dipped under. With a mighty heave, he lifted a large crappie into the air. Held at the utmost end of the line by centrifugal force, this fish described an arc that carried it thirty feet in the air. The man never stopped accelerating the pole until it extended behind him in the forest, and we could hear the fish flopping in the leaves far back in the woods. He dashed into the trees and fell upon it.

For years, just about everybody I fished with was a devotee of the South Sauty heave. My brother, in particular, thought it was a sin to lose a fish because of a broken line or to waste any time playing a fish. He was a believer in the old saw "First you get the fish in the boat, then you play with it." The heave, in short, was bred deeply into me.

*Images of trout fishing decorate fruit crate labels from the 1940s.*

I mention this here because I wish to discuss an essential stage of any fly-fishing career. In Canada, as I mentioned, I began learning to play heavy fish on a fly rod. After practicing on the three-pound bass that took the tiny popper on Minn Lake, I later landed and released a smallmouth of almost six pounds on Lac La Croix. But I was using strong leaders on those fish. Catching large trout on the almost invisible leaders, or tippets, required in very clear water is a more difficult matter.

Just how difficult I was to discover at an elbow-shaped pool on the Neshobe River near Brandon, Vermont. There for the first time I raised a sizable trout on a dry fly. It was a rainbow that darted from a deep whirl of current and gobbled the fly without ceremony. I set the hook sharply, and the fine tippet parted immediately. To say that this gave me a sinking feeling is accurate but does not capture exactly the quality of the moment.

When you are a beginner at fishing for trout in fast, clear water, you do not get many strikes like that. Most often, the fish see you because of your bad casting

*An exquisitely tied Joe's Hopper glistens in the sun. (Photograph © Erwin and Peggy Bauer)*

and clumsy wading, and they will not bite. Or your line gets caught in the current and jerks the fly along in a way that announces its fraudulent nature, and they do not bite because you have failed to achieve what the instructional booklets call "drag-free float." In any event, the uninhibited, get-hooked-or-be-damned strike of a substantial trout is a rare—indeed, for me at this stage, an unprecedented—event.

I am trying to communicate the profound feeling of stupidity that settled over me as I paced the gravel bar beside the pool and hurled curses into the genial summer sky. In psychological terms, I was contemplating the vast gap that lay between my knowledge and my behavior.

I knew, for example, that a trout will not strike a dry fly unless it is fished on a very fine tippet. I had tied my fly to such a tippet. I therefore knew that this tippet, by virtue of being thin to the point of near invisibility, was subject to the physical laws that govern our life on this planet.

*Warm tones evoke a solitary day's fishing in this painting by Ontario artist Richard Vander Meer.*

That is, I knew that it was not strong enough to drag a trout through the water against its will, much less lift it out onto the bank. All the same, I had given this fish the South Sauty heave.

The heave, of course, depends on those very same physical laws. That is, if you hook a large crappie—say, three pounds—and you are fishing with twenty-pound line, you can do what you like with that fish. You can, as my brother travelers on the Redneck Way are wont to say, "set the hook hard enough to cross his eyes."

But if you are after a three-pound trout on a two-pound line, *this will not work.* The fish in question punctuated this leap of cognition for me by dashing about the pool for a few moments, my fly clearly visible in the gristly joint of its jaw. This fish was well hooked, but it was not connected to me or, more precisely, to my several hundred dollars' worth of tackle that was *not capable of heaving a trout.*

That is how I came to understand the relationship between heavy fish and light lines. The act of setting the hook must contain within it an almost simultaneous act of surrender. Upon seeing or feeling the strike, the fly fisherman is required to pull back with precisely enough force to slide the point of the hook into the tissue of the fish's mouth. Then he must release all pressure and let the fish go where it wants to go. It is an act of physical discipline and of hope—the hope being that by and by when the fish is tired of going where it wants to go, it and the fisherman will still be connected by a thread that leads them to the same place.

This act of sliding home the hook and then bowing to the energy of the fish is easier to describe than to execute. It defines the difference between breaking rocks and cleaving diamonds. Mastery of this skill marks the line between those who are good at casting with a fly rod and those who are good at catching trout with a fly rod.

That day on the Neshobe, where the purple loosestrife bloomed in the meadow and tasseling corn whispered in the field, I was not optimistic about traversing that line. The eye-crossing hook set seemed embedded in the muscle memory of my right arm. I could feel it there when Ben and Jeff came hiking in from their beats on the Neshobe, fishless but full of teenage certainty that if that fish had hit *their* flies, it would have gotten defter play.

As it turned out, they were to break off their fair share of fish before we began to understand that the way to catch big trout was to give up in advance on the possibility of catching them. It was a matter of attitude, according to *A Modern Dry Fly Code*, published in 1950 by Vincent C. Marinaro, the arch-guru of Pennsylvania fly fishing. Forget about the actual landing of fish as a way of measuring your "luck," Marinaro advised, "for in the lexicon of the fly-fisherman, the words 'rise' and 'hooked' connote the successful and desirable climax; landing a fish is purely anticlimax."

A beautiful sentiment, I thought. But there was a self-evident flaw in the Higher Consciousness as defined by Marinaro. If you break off every good fish that rises to your fly, it leaves you feeling like a klutz. I had by this time begun to overcome my lust for fish, but I still lusted for expertise, for the feeling of artistry, for some control over the line-snapping reflex that lay coiled in my wrist, forearm and biceps.

Dick, as it turned out, knew quite a lot about Vince Marinaro. He made his living as a corporation-tax specialist for the State of Pennsylvania. The jacket photo on his book showed a wavy-haired, sharp-featured man in a tweed coat. He was looking, with a slightly sour expression, through a magnifying glass at a tiny fly. Marinaro's book, with its emphasis on fishing with impossibly small flies on the wispiest of leaders, had truly revolutionized American fly fishing, Dick said. But there were rumors that Marinaro died in 1986 an embittered man, feeling he never got the recognition he deserved. He left orders for his handmade bamboo fly rods to be burned.

"We ought to ask Charlie Fox about that the next time we go up to Cumberland County," he said, referring to the old man we had met on the banks of the Letort Spring Run on the day I caught my first trout.

It was on the Letort in the early 1950s that Marinaro and Fox had coached a young architect named Ernest Schwiebert in the learning that went into *Matching the Hatch*. The books by Marinaro and Schwiebert, Dick said, established the superiority of American fly fishing over its British antecedent. Fox himself had written a book, *The Wonderful World of Trout*, that also showed up occasionally on the outdoor magazines' lists of the ten best books about American fly fishing. In short, in Marinaro, Schwiebert and Fox on the Letort, you had something like the fly-fishing equivalent of Hemingway, Fitzgerald and Dos Passos in Paris.

"The one quantum leap I made last year was on the Letort. I describe it as 'beyond barbless,' " Dick said. "I went up last February and I was fishing for these big browns with Shenk's Sculpins, and I tell you I was knocking them dead. I finally decided that the fun was not in landing the fish. The fun was in seeing the fish take. So I began cutting my Sculpins right at the bend of the hook, and they would grab it, and I would just jerk it out of their mouth, except that one time a fish grabbed it, and I pulled him up on the bank. He wouldn't let go. I guess I decided that in a number of situations as long as I can see the fish take, I'd just as soon not have the hook on. I could go out here on a blue-ribbon trout stream, and I could do that with a dry fly because it would be the take that would give me the thrill."

I was not ready for "beyond barbless," nor for the abnegation of Vince Marinaro. But as a political reporter, I had learned to be patient when being lectured or lied to and to look for the lesson lurking beneath the bombast. What would happen, for example, if upon raising a trout one immediately feigned indifference to its capture? What if one set out not to land the fish, but simply to prevent it from breaking the line?

I had plenty of time to contemplate that question, for it seemed that after I broke off that fish on the Neshobe I had hit a kind of plateau. I no longer enjoyed Glo Bug fishing, but I was not very good at anything else. The confidence that had bloomed in Canada and among the innocent wild brookies of the Rapidan began to wither. One hot Sunday afternoon, Ben and I went to Big Hunting Creek. I was making my way from pool to pool with clumsy perfunctory casts, feeling neither confidence nor hope, when I threw an Elk Hair Caddis into a dark pool at the foot of a small waterfall. A trout came up instantly, and something happened there that I did not will or control. It was if a kind of synaptic switch had flopped over in my brain and I experienced the strike of this trout in slow motion, just as on the less demanding water in Canada. Instead of setting the hook with a furious jerk of my rod, I raised it smoothly, and once I had put the hook home, I relented and let the fish go where it liked, exerting just enough pressure to make the line tight and to pull a nice bow in my rod.

The fish zoomed upstream, making my drag sing. Reaching the limit of the pool, it came back down toward me until it reached the tail of the pool. Then it took off again toward the upper end, again making my reel sing its mechanical song. Next the fish dove to the bottom of the pool, and I could feel the biggest brown trout I had ever hooked butting its head against the rocks, and I thought certainly it would rub the leader in two. But all I could do was choose between breaking the line or letting the fish have its way for a while. So I let the fish go where it wanted to go until it was so tired that it had to go where my rod and line wanted it to go, which was into my hand.

*"The strongest impressions on my mind are of the last casts in the twilight."—William Cowper Prime, I Go a-Fishing, 1873 (Photograph © Dennis Frates)*

I laid it on the wet gravel and photographed it, a brown trout of astonishing beauty. I had just released the fish when Ben came bursting through the trees.

"Was that your drag I heard?" he said.

I said it was, and for once, I understood what it was saying. It was telling me that the only way to land a big fish is to submit to its power, especially at the strike and in the early moments of the hookup when it is throwing raw energy every which way.

Later, I learned there was a name for what I had done. It is called "throwing slack." As Lefty Kreh explains in *Lefty's Little Library of Fly Fishing*, "It's the jerk of the leader that breaks the line. So after I set the hook, I always throw a little bit of slack."

Being an English major, I knew that Mr. Yeats had said it better in "The Three Beggars":

> It's certain there are trout somewhere
> And maybe I shall take a trout
> If but I do not seem to care.

# The River God

*By Roland Pertwee*

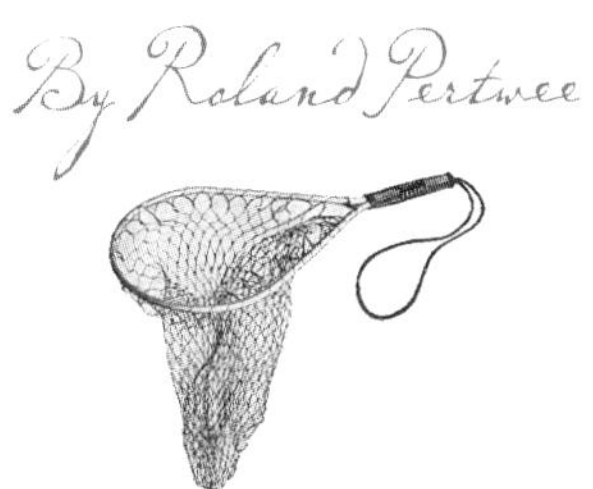

A native of Brighton, England, Roland Pertwee (1885-1963) was a prolific playwright, screen writer, novelist, and storywriter. In 1928, his play *Interference* hit the London and New York stages with resounding success. Later works include *Dinner at the Ritz* (1937), *Pink String and Sealing Wax* (1943), and *Not Wanted on Voyage* (1957).

Pertwee also wrote an autobiography, *Master to None* (1940), in which he depicts himself as a jack-of-all-trades but a master of none. Readers of his short stories would beg to differ. A deft writer of scene and dialogue, Pertwee published his short prose in magazines such as the *Saturday Evening Post* and *Strand*. He was a devotee of the genre and wrote until the week he died.

This story, a perennial favorite since its publication in 1951, beautifully dramatizes a boy's initiation into the seductive sport of fly fishing.

LEFT: *Under a gorgeous Idaho sky, an angler swirls his fly line over a pond in Sawtooth National Recreational Area. (Photograph © Dennis Frates)*

*Nostalgic fly fishing artwork adorns these collectible 1950s ink blotters from Mac's Thrifty Store in Athens, Ohio.*

WHEN I WAS a little boy I had a friend who was a colonel. He was not the kind of colonel you meet nowadays, who manages a motor showroom in the West End of London and wears crocodile shoes and a small moustache and who calls you "old man" and slaps your back, independent of the fact that you may have been no more than a private in the war. My colonel was of the older order that takes a third of a century and a lot of Indian sun and Madras curry in the making. A veteran of the Mutiny he was, and wore side whiskers to prove it. Once he came upon a number of Sepoys conspiring mischief in a byre with a barrel of gunpowder. So he put the butt of his cheroot into the barrel and presently they all went to hell. That was the kind of man he was in the way of business.

In the way of pleasure he was very different. In the way of pleasure he wore an old Norfolk coat that smelled of heather and brine, and which had no elbows to speak of. And he wore a Sherlock Holmesy kind of cap with a swarm of salmon flies upon it, that to my boyish fancy was more splendid than a crown. I cannot remember his legs, because they were nearly always under water, hidden in great canvas waders. But once he sent me a photograph of himself riding on a tricycle, so I expect he had some knickerbockers, too, which would have been that tight kind, with a box cloth under the knees. Boys don't take much stock of clothes. His head occupied my imagination. A big, brave, white-haired head with cheery-red rugose cheeks and honest, laughing, puckered eyes, with gunpowder marks in their corners.

People at the little Welsh fishing inn where we met said he was a bore; but I knew him to be a god and shall prove it.

I was ten years old and his best friend. He was seventy something and my hero.

Properly I should not have mentioned my hero so soon in this narrative. He belongs to a later epoch, but sometimes it is forgivable to start with a boast, and now that I have committed myself I lack the courage to call upon my colonel to fall back two paces to the rear, quick march, and wait until he is wanted.

The real beginning takes place, as I remember, somewhere in Hampshire on the Grayshott Road, among sandy banks, sentinel firs, and plum-colored wastes of heather. Summer-holiday time it was, and I was among folks whose names have since vanished like lizards under the stones of forgetfulness. Perhaps it was a picnic walk; perhaps I carried a basket and was told not to swing it for fear of bursting its cargo of ginger beer. In those days ginger beer had big bulgy corks held down with a string. In a hot sun or under stress of too much agitation the string would break and the corks fly. Then there would be a merry foaming fountain and someone would get reproached.

One of our company had a fishing rod. He was a young man who, one day, was to be an uncle of mine. But that didn't concern me. What concerned me was the fishing rod and presently—perhaps because he felt he must keep in with the family—he let me carry it. To the fisherman born there is nothing so provoking of curiosity as a fishing rod in a case.

Surreptitiously I opened the flap, which contained a small grass spear in a wee pocket, and, pulling down the case a little, I admired the beauties of the work butt, with its gun-metal ferrule and reel rings and the exquisite frail slenderness of the two top joints.

"It's got two top joints—two!" I exclaimed ecstatically. "Of course," said he. "All good trout rods have two."

I marveled in silence at what seemed to me then a combination of extravagance and excellent precaution.

There must have been something inherently understanding and noble about that young man who would one day be my uncle, for, taking me by the arm, he sat me down on a tuft of heather and took the pieces of rod from the case and fitted them together. The rest of the company moved on and left me in Paradise.

It is thirty-five years ago since that moment and not one detail of it is forgotten. There sounds in my ears today as clearly as then, the faint, clear pop made by the little cork stoppers with their boxwood tops as they were withdrawn. I remember how, before fitting the pieces together, he rubbed the ferrules against the side of his nose to prevent them sticking. I remember looking up the length of it through a tunnel of sneck rings to the eyelet at the end. Not until he had fixed a reel and passed a line through the rings did he put the lovely thing into my hand. So light it was, so firm, so persuasive; such a thing alive—a scepter. I could do no more than say, "Oo!" and again, "Oo!"

"A thrill, ain't it?" said he.

I had no need to answer that. In my new-found rapture was only one sorrow, the knowledge that such happiness would not endure and that, all too soon, a blank and rodless future awaited me.

"They must be awfully—awfully 'spensive," I said.

"Couple of guineas," he replied offhandedly.

A couple of guineas! And we were poor folk and the future was more rodless than ever.

"Then I shall save and save and save," I said.

*The rushing waters of Oregon's North Umpqua River teem with salmon and steelhead during spawning season. (Photograph © Dennis Frates)*

And my imagination started to add up twopence a week into guineas. Two hundred and forty pennies to the pound, multiplied by two—four hundred and eighty—and then another twenty-four pennies—five hundred and four. Why, it would take a lifetime, and no sweets, no elastic for catapults, no penny novelty boxes or airgun bullets or ices or anything. Tragedy must have been writ large upon my face, for he said suddenly, "When's your birthday?"

I was almost ashamed to tell him how soon it was. Perhaps he, too, was a little taken aback by its proximity, for that future uncle of mine was not so rich as uncles should be.

"We must see about it."

"But it wouldn't—it couldn't be one like that," I said.

I must have touched his pride, for he answered loftily, "Certainly it will."

In the fortnight that followed I walked on air and told everybody I had as good as got a couple-of-guineas rod.

*This undated historical photograph captures a dramatic moment against a beautiful mountain vista. (Courtesy of the Colorado Historical Society)*

No one can deceive a child, save the child himself, and when my birthday came and with it a long brown-paper parcel, I knew, even before I had removed the wrappers, that this two-guineas rod was not worth the money. There was a brown linen case, it is true, but it was not a case with a neat compartment for each joint, nor was there a spear in the flap. There was only one top instead of two, and there were no popping little stoppers to protect the ferrules from dust and injury. The lower joint boasted no elegant cork hand piece, but was a tapered affair coarsely made and rudely varnished. When I fitted the pieces together, what I balanced in my hand was tough and stodgy, rather than limber. The reel, which had come in a different parcel, was of wood. It had neither check nor brake, and the line overran and backwound itself with distressing frequency.

I had not read and reread Gamages' price list without knowing something of rods, and I did not need to look long at this rod before realizing that it was no match to the one I had handled on the Grayshott Road.

I believe at first a great sadness possessed me, but very presently imagination came to the rescue. For I told myself that I had only to think that this was the rod of all other rods that I desired most and it would be so. And it was so.

Furthermore, I told myself that, in this great wide ignorant world, but few people existed with such expert knowledge of rods as I possessed. That I had but to say, "Here is the final word in good rods," and they would accept it as such.

Very confidently I tried the experiment on my mother, with inevitable success. From the depths of her affection and her ignorance on all such matters, she produced:

"It's a magnificent rod."

I went my way, knowing full well that she knew not what she said, but that she was kind.

With rather less confidence I approached my father, saying, "Look, father! It cost two guineas. It's absolutely the best sort you can get."

And he, after waggling it a few moments in silence, quoted cryptically: "There is nothing either good or bad but thinking makes it so."

Young as I was, I had some curiosity about words, and on any other occasion I would have called on him to explain. But this I did not do, but left hurriedly, for fear that he should explain.

In the two years that followed, I fished every day in the slip of a back garden of our tiny London house. And, having regard to the fact that this rod was never fashioned to throw a fly, I acquired a pretty knack in the fullness of time and performed some glib casting at the nasturtiums and marigolds that flourished by the back wall.

My parents' fortunes must have been in the ascendant, I suppose, for I call to mind an unforgettable breakfast when my mother told me that father had decided we should spend our summer holiday at a Welsh hotel on the river Lledr. The place was called Pont-y-pant, and she showed me a picture of the hotel with a great knock-me-down river creaming past the front of it.

Although in my dreams I had heard fast water often enough, I had never seen it, and the knowledge that in a month's time I should wake with the music of a cataract in my ears was almost more than patience could endure.

In that exquisite, intolerable period of suspense I suffered as only childish longing and enthusiasm can suffer. Even the hand of gut that I bought and bent into innumerable casts failed to alleviate that suffering. I would walk for miles for a moment's delight captured in gluing my nose to the windows of tackleists' shops in the West End. I learned from my grandmother—a wise and calm old lady—how to make nets and, having mastered the art, I made myself a landing net. This I set up on a frame fashioned from a penny schoolmaster's cane bound to an old walking stick. It would be pleasant to record that this was a good and serviceable net, but it was not. It flopped over in a very distressing fashion when called upon to lift the lightest weight. I had to confess to myself that I had more enthusiasm than skill in the manufacture of such articles.

At school there was a boy who had a fishing creel, which he swapped with me for a Swedish knife, a copy of Rogues of the Fiery Cross, and an Easter egg I had kept on account of its rare beauty. He had forced a hard bargain and was sure he had the best of it, but I knew otherwise.

At last the great day dawned, and after infinite travel by train we reached our destination as the glow of sunset was graying into dark. The river was in spate, and as we crossed a tall stone bridge on our way to the hotel I heard it below me, barking and grumbling among great rocks. I was pretty far gone in tiredness, for I remember little else that night but a rod rack in the hall—a dozen rods of different sorts and sizes, with gaudy salmon flies, some nets, a gaff, and an oak coffer upon which lay a freshly caught salmon on a blue ashet. Then supper by candlelight, bed, a glitter of stars through the open window, and the ceaseless drumming of water.

By six o'clock next morning I was on the river bank, fitting my rod together and watching in awe the great brown ribbon of water go fleetly by.

Among my most treasured possessions were half a dozen flies, and two of these I attached to the cast with exquisite care. While so engaged, a shadow fell on the grass beside me and looking up, I beheld a lank, shabby individual with a walrus moustache and an unhealthy face, who, the night before, had helped with our luggage at the station.

"Water's too heavy for flies," said he, with an uptilting inflection. "This evening, yes; now, no—none whateffer. Better try with a worrum in the burrun."

He pointed at a busy little brook that tumbled down the steep hillside and joined the main stream at the garden end.

"C-couldn't I fish with a fly in the—the burrun?" I asked, for although I wanted to catch a fish very badly, for honor's sake I would fain take it on a fly.

*"Coming to Net - Atlantic Salmon," an original oil painting by sporting artist Eldridge Hardie, evokes the companionship of a day on the river. Hardie's paintings have been exhibited in the National Museum of Wildlife Art, the American Museum of Fly Fishing, and—in a one-man retrospective—the National Bird Dog Museum.*

"Indeed, no," he replied, slanting the tone of his voice skyward. "You cootn't. Neffer. And that isn't a fly rod whateffer."

"It is," I replied hotly. "Yes, it is."

But he only shook his head and repeated, "No," and took the rod from my hand and illustrated its awkwardness and handed it back with a wretched laugh.

If he had pitched me into the river I should have been happier.

"It is a fly rod and it cost two guineas," I said, and my lower lip trembled.

"Neffer," he repeated. "Five shillings would be too much."

Even a small boy is entitled to some dignity.

Picking up my basket, I turned without another word and made for the hotel. Perhaps my eyes were blinded with tears, for I was about to plunge into the dark hall when a great, rough, kindly voice arrested me with:

"Easy does it."

At the thick end of an immense salmon rod there strode out into the sunlight the noblest figure I had ever seen.

There is no real need to describe my colonel again—I have done so already—but the temptation is too great. Standing in the doorway, the sixteen-foot rod in hand, the deerstalker hat, besprent with flies, crowning his shaggy head, the waders, like seven-league boots, braced up to his armpits, the creel across his shoulder, a gaff across his back, he looked what he was—a god. His eyes met mine with that kind of smile one good man keeps for another.

*Minnesota artist Bob White painted this artful study of a Chinook salmon. Also a photographer, hunter, and renowned fly fishing guide, White works from his home in Marine on St. Croix, Minnesota.*

"An early start," he said. "Any luck, old feller?"

I told him I hadn't started—not yet.

"Wise chap," said he. "Water's a bit heavy for trouting. It'll soon run down, though. Let's vet those flies of yours."

He took my rod and whipped it expertly. "A nice piece—new, eh?"

"N-not quite," I stammered; "but I haven't used it yet, sir, in water."

That god read men's minds.

"I know, garden practice; capital; nothing like it."

Releasing my cast, he frowned critically over the flies—a Blue Dun and a March Brown.

"Think so?" he queried. "You don't think it's a shade late in the season for these fancies?" I said I thought perhaps it was.

"Yes, I think you're right," said he. "I believe in this big water you'd do better with a livelier pattern. Teal and Red, Cock-y-bundy, Greenwell's Glory." I said nothing, but nodded gravely at these brave names.

Once more he read my thoughts and saw through the wicker sides of my creel a great emptiness.

"I expect you've fished most in southern rivers. These Welsh trout have a fancy for a spot of color."

He rummaged in the pocket of his Norfolk jacket and produced a round tin which once had held saddle soap.

"Collar on to that," said he, "there's a proper pickle of flies and casts in that.

As a keen fisherman, you don't mind sorting 'em out. They may come in useful."

"But, I say, you don't mean—" I began.

"Yes, go on; stick to it. All fishermen are members of the same club and I'm giving the trout a rest for a bit." His eyes ranged the hills and trees opposite. "I must be getting on with it before the sun's too high."

Waving his free hand, he strode away and presently was lost to view at a bend in the road.

I think my mother was a little piqued by my abstraction during breakfast. My eyes never, for an instant, deserted the round tin box that lay open beside my plate. Within it were a paradise and a hundred miracles all tangled together in the pleasantest disorder. My mother said something about a lovely walk over the hills, but I had other plans, which included a very glorious hour that should be spent untangling and wrapping up in neat squares of paper my new treasures.

"I suppose he knows best what he wants to do," she said.

So it came about that I was left alone and betook myself to a sheltered spot behind a rock where all the delicious disorder was remedied and I could take stock of what was mine.

I am sure there were at least six casts all set up with flies, and ever so many loose flies and one great stout, tapered cast, with a salmon fly upon it, that was so rich in splendor that I doubted if my benefactor could really have known that it was there.

I felt almost guilty at owning so much, and not until I had done full justice to everything did I fasten a new cast to my line and go a-fishing.

There is a lot said and written about beginner's luck, but none of it came my way. Indeed, I spent most of the morning extricating my line from the most fearsome tangles. I had no skill in throwing a cast with two droppers upon it and I found it was an art not to be learned in a minute. Then, from overeagerness, I was too snappy with my back cast, whereby, before many minutes had gone, I heard that warning crack behind me that betokens the loss of a tail fly. I must have spent half an hour searching the meadow for that lost fly and finding it not. Which is not strange, for I wonder has any fisherman ever found that lost fly. The reeds, the buttercups and the little people with many legs who run in the wet grass conspire together to keep the secret of its hiding place. I gave up at last, and with a feeling of shame that was only proper, I invested a new fly on the point of my cast and set to work again, but more warily.

In that hard racing water a good strain was put upon my rod, and before the morning was out it was creaking at the joints in a way that kept my heart continually in my mouth. It is the duty of a rod to work with a single smooth action and by no means to divide its performance into three sections of activity. It is a hard task for any angler to persuade his line austerely if his rod behaves thus.

When, at last, my father strolled up the river bank, walking, to his shame, much nearer the water than a good fisherman should, my nerves were jumpy from apprehension.

"Come along. Food's ready. Done any good?" said he.

Again it was to his discredit that he put food before sport, but I told him I had had a wonderful morning, and he was glad.

"What do you want to do this afternoon, old man?" he asked.

"Fish," I said.

"But you can't always fish," he said.

I told him I could and I was right and have proved it for thirty years and more.

"Well, well," he said, "please yourself, but isn't it dull not catching anything?"

And I said, as I've said a thousand times since, "As if it could be."

So that afternoon I went downstream instead of up, and found myself in difficult country where the river boiled between the narrows of two hills. Stunted oaks overhung the water and great boulders opposed its flow. Presently I came to a sort of natural flight of steps—a pool and a cascade three times repeated—and there, watching the maniac fury of the waters in awe and wonderment, I saw the most stirring sight in my young life. I saw a silver salmon leap superbly from the cauldron below into the pool above. And I saw another and another salmon do likewise. And I wonder the eyes of me did not fall out of my head.

I cannot say how long I stayed watching that gallant pageant of leaping fish—in ecstasy there is no measurement of time—but at last it came upon me that all the salmon in the sea were careering past me and that if I were to realize my soul's desire I must hasten to the pool below before the last of them had gone by.

It was a mad adventure, for until I had discovered that stout cast, with the gaudy fly attached in the tin box, I had given no thought to such noble quarry. My recent possessions had put ideas into my head above my station and beyond my powers. Failure, however, means little to the young, and walking fast, yet gingerly, for fear of breaking my rod top against a tree, I followed the path downstream until I came to a great basin of water into which, through a narrow throat, the river thundered like a storm.

At the head of the pool was a plate of rocks scored by the nails of fishermen's boots, and here I sat down to wait while the salmon cast, removed from its wrapper, was allowed to soak and soften in a puddle left by the rain.

And while I waited a salmon rolled not ten yards from where I sat. Head and tail, up and down he went, a great monster of a fish, sporting and deriding me.

With that performance so near at hand, I have often wondered how I was able to control my fingers well enough to tie a figure-eight knot between the line and the cast. But I did, and I'm proud to be able to record it. Your true-born angler does not go blindly to work until he has first satisfied his con-

*An fly fisherman returns an Atlantic salmon to its home, the catch-and-release-only Ponoi River in Russia. (Photograph © R. Valentine Atkinson)*

*Low sunlight bathes an angler selecting flies to try on Henry's Fork of the Snake River. (Photograph © R. Valentine Atkinson)*

science. There is a pride in knots, of which the laity knows nothing, and if, through neglect to tie them rightly, failure and loss should result, pride may not be restored nor conscience salved by the plea of eagerness. With my trembling fingers I bent the knot and, with a pummeling heart, launched the line into the broken water at the throat of the pool.

At first the mere tug of the water against that large fly was so thrilling to me that it was hard to believe that I had not hooked a whale. The trembling line swung round in a wide arc into a calm eddy below where I stood. Before casting afresh I shot a glance over my shoulder to assure myself there was no limb of a tree behind me to foul the fly. And this was a gallant cast, true and straight, with a couple of yards more length than its predecessor, and a wider radius. Instinctively I knew, as if the surface had been marked with an X where the salmon had risen, that my fly must pass right over the spot. As it swung by, my nerves were strained like piano wires. I think I knew that something tremendous, impossible, terrifying, was going to happen. The sense, the certitude was so strong in me that I half opened my mouth to shout a warning to the monster, not to.

I must have felt very, very young in that moment. I, who that same day had been talked to as a man by a man among men. The years were stripped from me and I was what I was—ten years old and appalled. And then, with the suddenness of a rocket, it happened. The water was cut into a swathe. I remember a silver loop bearing downward—a bright, shining, vanishing thing like the bobbin of my mother's sewing machine—and a tug. I shall never forget the viciousness of that tug. I had my fingers tight upon the line, so I got the full force of it. To counteract a tendency to go headfirst into the spinning water below, I threw myself backward and sat down on the hard rock with a jar that shut my teeth on my tongue—like the jaws of a trap.

Luckily I had let the rod go out straight with the line, else it must have snapped in the first frenzy of the downstream rush. Little ass that I was, I tried to check the speeding line with my forefinger, with the result that it cut and burnt me to the bone. There wasn't above twenty yards of line in the reel, and the wretched contrivance was trying to be rid of the line even faster than the fish was wrenching it out. Heaven knows why it didn't snarl, for great loops and whorls were whirling like Catherine wheels, under my wrist. An instant's glance revealed the terrifying fact that there were not more than half a dozen yards left on the reel and the fish showed no signs of abating his rush. With the realization of impending and inevitable catastrophe upon me, I launched a yell for help, which, rising above the roar of the waters, went echoing down the gorge.

And then, to add to my terrors, the salmon leaped—a winging leap like a silver arch appearing and instantly disappearing upon the broken surface. So mighty, so all-powerful he seemed in that sublime moment that I lost all sense of reason and raised the rod, with a sudden jerk, above my head.

I have often wondered, had the rod actually been the two-guinea rod my imagination claimed for it, whether it could have withstood the strain thus violently and unreasonably imposed upon it. The wretched thing that I held so grimly never even put up a fight. It snapped at the ferrule of the lower joint and plunged like a toboggan down the slanting line, to vanish into the black depths of the water.

My horror at this calamity was so profound that I was lost even to the consciousness that the last of my line had run out. A couple of vicious tugs advised me of this awful truth. Then, snap! The line parted at the reel, flickered out through the rings and was gone. I was left with nothing but the butt of a broken rod in my hand and an agony of mind that even now I cannot recall without emotion.

I am not ashamed to confess that I cried. I lay down on the rock, with my cheek in the puddle where I had soaked the cast, and plenished it with my tears. For what had the future left for me but a cut and burning finger, a badly bumped behind, the single joint of a broken rod and no faith in uncles? How long I lay there weeping I do not know. Ages, perhaps, or minutes, or seconds.

I was roused by a rough hand on my shoulder and a kindly voice demanding, "Hurt yourself, Ike Walton?"

Blinking away my tears, I pointed at my broken rod with a bleeding forefinger.

"Come! This is bad luck," said my colonel, his face grave as a stone. "How did it happen?"

"I c-caught a s-salmon."

"You what?" said he.

"I d-did," I said.

He looked at me long and earnestly; then, taking my injured hand, he looked at that and nodded.

"The poor groundlings who can find no better use for a river than something to put a bridge over think all fishermen are liars," said he. "But we know better, eh? By the bumps and breaks and cuts I'd say you made a plucky fight against heavy odds. Let's hear all about it."

So, with his arm round my shoulders and his great shaggy head near to mine, I told him all about it.

At the end he gave me a mighty and comforting squeeze, and he said, "The loss of one's first big fish is the heaviest loss I know. One feels, whatever happens, one'll never—" He stopped and pointed dramatically. "There it goes—see! Down there at the tail of the pool!"

In the broken water where the pool emptied itself into the shallows beyond, I saw the top joints of my rod dancing on the surface.

"Come on!" he shouted, and gripping my hand, jerked me to my feet. "Scatter your legs! There's just a chance!"

Dragging me after him, we raced along by the river path to the end of the pool, where, on a narrow promontory of grass, his enormous salmon rod was lying.

"Now," he said, picking it up and making the line whistle to and fro in the air with sublime authority, "keep your eyes skinned on those shallows for another glimpse of it."

A second later I was shouting, "There! There!"

He must have seen the rod point at the same moment, for his line flowed out and the big fly hit the water with a plop not a couple of feet from the spot. He let it ride on the current, playing it with a sensitive touch like the brushwork of an artist.

"Half a jiffy!" he exclaimed at last. "Wait! Yes, I think so. Cut down to that rock and see if I haven't fished up the line."

I needed no second invitation, and presently was yelling, "Yes—yes, you have!"

"Stretch yourself out then and collar hold of it."

With the most exquisite care he navigated the line to where I lay stretched upon the rock. Then:

"Right you are! Good lad! I'm coming down."

Considering his age, he leaped the rocks like a chamois.

"Now," he said, and took the wet line delicately between his forefinger and thumb. One end trailed limply downstream, but the other end seemed anchored in the big pool where I had had my unequal and disastrous contest.

Looking into his face, I saw a sudden light of excitement dancing in his eyes. "Odd," he muttered, "but not impossible."

"What isn't?" I asked breathlessly.

"Well, it looks to me as if the top joints of that rod of yours have gone downstream."

Gingerly he pulled up the line, and presently an end with a broken knot appeared.

"The reel knot, eh?" I nodded gloomily. "Then we lose the rod," said he. That wasn't very heartening news. "On the other hand, it's just possible the fish is still on—sulking."

"Oh!" I exclaimed.

"Now, steady does it," he warmed, "and give me my rod."

Taking a pair of clippers from his pocket, he cut his own line just above the cast.

"Can you tie a knot?" he asked.

"Yes," I nodded.

"Come on, then; bend your line on to mine. Quick as lightning."

Under his critical eye, I joined the two lines with a blood knot. "I guessed you were a fisherman," he said, nodded approvingly and clipped off the ends. "And now to know the best or the worst."

I shall never forget the music of that check reel or the suspense with which I watched as, with the butt of the rod bearing against the hollow of his thigh, he steadily wound up the wet slack line. Every instant I expected it to come drifting downstream, but it didn't. Presently it rose in a tight slant from the pool above.

"Snagged, I'm afraid," he said, and worked the rod with an easy straining motion to and fro. "Yes, I'm afraid—no, by Lord Bobs, he's on!"

I think it was only right and proper that I should have launched a yell of triumph as, with the spoken word, the point at which the line cut the water shifted magically from the left side of the pool to the right.

"And a fish too," said he.

In the fifteen minutes that followed, I must have experienced every known form of terror and delight.

"Youngster," said he, "you should be doing this, by rights, but I'm afraid the rod's a bit above your weight."

"Oh, go on and catch him," I pleaded.

"And so I will," he promised; "unship the gaff, young 'un, and stand by to use it, and if you break the cast we'll never speak to each other again, and that's a bet."

But I didn't break the cast. The noble, courageous, indomitable example of my river god had lent me skill and precision beyond my years. When at long last a weary, beaten, silver monster rolled within reach of my arm into a shallow eddy, the steel gaff shot out fair and true, and sank home.

And then I was lying on the grass, with my arms round a salmon that weighed twenty-two pounds on the scale and contained every sort of happiness known to a boy.

And best of all, my river god shook hands with me and called me "partner."

That evening the salmon was placed upon the blue ashet in the hall, bearing a little card with its weight and my name upon it.

And I am afraid I sat on a chair facing it, for ever so long, so that I could hear what the other anglers had to say as they passed by. I was sitting there when my colonel put his head out of his private sitting room and beckoned me to come in.

"A true fisherman lives in the future, not the past, old man," said he; "though, for this once, it 'ud be a shame to reproach you."

I suppose I colored guiltily—at any rate I hope so.

"We got the fish," said he, "but we lost the rod, and the future without a rod doesn't bear thinking of. Now"—and he pointed at a long wooden box on the floor, that overflowed with rods of different sorts and sizes—"rummage among those. Take your time and see if you can find anything to suit you."

"But do you mean—can I?"

"We're partners, aren't we? And p'r'aps as such you'd rather we went through our stock together."

"Oo, sir," I said.

"Here, quit that," he ordered gruffly. "By Lord Bobs, if a show like this afternoon's don't deserve a medal, what does? Now, here's a handy piece by Hardy—a light and useful tool—or if you fancy greenheart in preference to split bamboo—"

I have the rod to this day, and I count it among my dearest treasures. And to this day I have a flick of the wrist that was his legacy. I have, too, some small skill in dressing flies, the elements of which were learned in his company by candle-

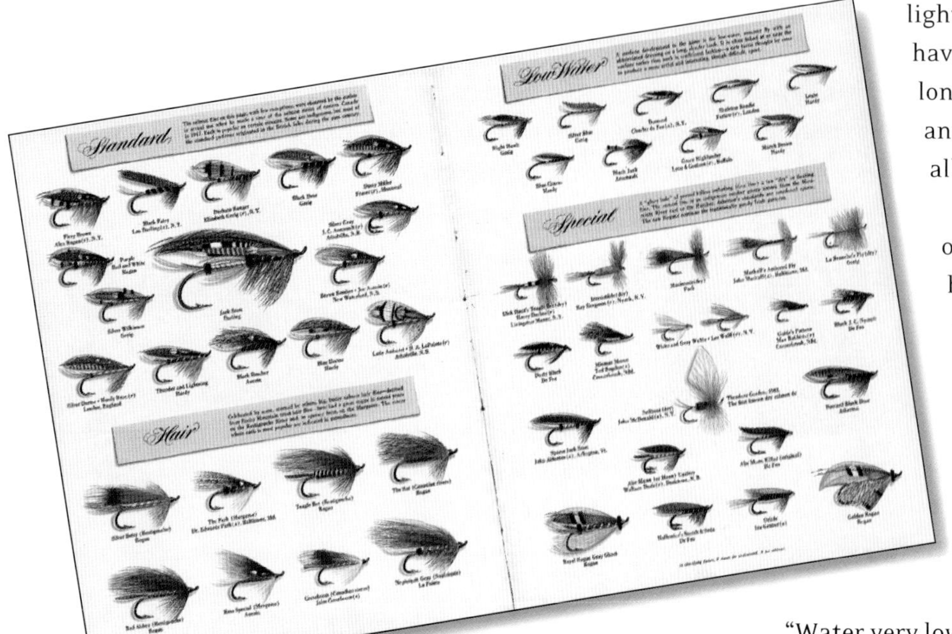


*Spawning salmon ought beware "the angler, who presents dangerous little baubles of tinsels and plumage—salmon flies—for his attention." Dating from the 1940s, this magazine page presents a dazzling variety of "baubles."*

light after the day's work was over. And I have countless memories of that month-long, month-short friendship—the closest and most perfect friendship, perhaps, of all my life.

He came to the station and saw me off. How I vividly remember his shaggy head at the window, with the whiskered cheeks and the gunpowder marks at the comers of his eyes! I didn't cry, although I wanted to awfully. We were partners and shook hands. I never saw him again, although on my birthdays I would have colored cards from him, with Irish, Scotch, Norwegian postmarks. Very brief they were: "Water very low." "Took a good fish last Thursday." "Been prawning but don't like it."

Sometimes at Christmas I had gifts—a reel, a tapered line, a fly book. But I never saw him again.

Came at last no more postcards or gifts, but in the *Fishing Gazette*, of which I was a religious reader, was an obituary telling how one of the last of the Mutiny veterans had joined the great majority. It seems he had been fishing half an hour before he died. He had taken his rod down and passed out. They had buried him at Totnes, overlooking the River Dart.

So he was no more—my river god—and what was left of him they had put into a box and buried it in the earth.

But that isn't true; nor is it true that I never saw him again. For I seldom go a-fishing but that I meet him on the river banks.

The banks of a river are frequented by a strange company and are full of mysterious and murmurous sounds—the cluck and laughter of water, the piping of birds, the hum of insects and the whispering of wind in the willows. What should prevent a man in such a place having a word and speech with another who is not there? So much of fishing lies in imagination, and mine needs little stretching to give my river god a living form.

"With this ripple," says he, "you should do well."

"And what's it to be," say I— "Blue Upright, Red Spinner? What's your fancy, sir?"

Spirits never grow old. He has begun to take an interest in dry-fly methods—that river god of mine, with his seven-league boots, his shaggy head and the gaff across his back.

*Father and son get an early morning start fly-fishing in Yellowstone National Park. (Photograph © Jeff Henry/Roche Jaune Pictures, Inc.)*

# I'm No Ted Williams

By Charles Elliott

Georgia native Charles Newton Elliott (1906–2000) attained national status for his expertise in forestry and the outdoors. Variously a ranger for his home state and the National Park Service, Elliott is immortalized in several ways. First—and fittingly—the Georgia Department of Natural Resources preserves his legacy with the six-acre Charlie Elliott Wildlife Center in Monticello. A more obscure legacy is the "Mark Trail" comic strip, which cartoonist and fellow Georgian Ed Dodd based on Elliott's life as a forest ranger and outdoors writer.

Elliott was indeed a talented and prolific writer, penning countless articles for sporting magazines. He also wrote dozens of textbooks on outdoors subjects, as well the autobiographical *Gone Fishin'* (1953), *Gone Huntin'* (1954), and *An Outdoor Life* (1994).

As field editor of *Outdoor Life* for nearly twenty years, Elliott often hunted and fished with prominent sportsmen. Here, he gets a lesson in bonefish angling from baseball great Ted Williams.

LEFT: *A saltwater fisherman's legs disappear into the crystalline waters of the Belize flats. (Photograph © Doug Stamm)*

I CAN DEPOSIT a fly that weighs no more than thistledown on any square foot of a trout pool, or drop a plug through an opening at the base of a cypress, to entice the old bass there into a slashing strike. Once, after trailing a ram for two days along a high divide, I shot him just as he jumped for the protection of the rim-rock wall. And another time I stood in my tracks and broke the neck of a charging grizzly.

But never, either with a rod or with a gun, have I found a tougher challenge than the precise shot of the fly to a cruising bonefish.

A bonefish is, by no stretch of the imagination, a large or even a vicious creature. The world record on rod and reel is sixteen pounds. Yet I have seen strong men, who could flyrod a tarpon as big as an umpire without breaking a bead of sweat turn pale at the sight of an eight-pound bonefish moving at a walk through the water.

Joe Brooks, manager of the Metropolitan Miami Fishing Tournament, tried to explain it to me, and so did Ted Williams, one of baseball's immortals. It has something to do, they said, with the fact that in bonefishing a man must cast quickly and accurately to a specific target he can see, whereas in other kinds of fishing he's throwing blind, hoping for the best.

It combines both fishing and hunting where a man has to have eyes like an osprey, arms like the village blacksmith, and a shooting eye like Annie Oakley's—where wind and sun and a weed-and-limestone bottom conspire to help the fish instead of the angler.

"All you have to do," Ted explained, waving his hamlike paws at me, "is keep calm. Just don't get excited."

He was so serious that I wanted to laugh. Who could get excited about a fish in the ten-pound class? I'd had tarpon jump into the rowboat with me, and caught channel bass that could have flipped us over with a thrust of the tail. But I nodded solemnly and felt the powerful backbone of the plastic-impregnated rod Joe put in my hands. The big salmon reel on the butt end was equipped with a G-A-F line and 200 yards of backing.

*Small in size but not in strength, this silvery bonefish was caught on a Mini Puff. (Photograph © Doug Stamm)*

"Why this?" I asked, putting my finger on the reel.

Joe grinned. "Wait till you hook one of those babies. You'll find out."

We were on the outer reefs between the broad Atlantic and the mangrove island flanking Key Largo. Bonefish come out of the deep water to feed on these shallow flats around the points and in the deep indentations of the bays. It is one of the most productive places on the upper Florida keys for bonefish.

"Sure you can handle that rod?" Ted asked.

I grunted a reply and shot out sixty feet behind the torpedo head to show him I was familiar with the technique of a heavy fly rod.

"If you'd add another forty feet to that, it wouldn't hurt," he said.

Everything must be right in order to see, hook, and land a bonefish. We had

*Anglers linger till sunset in the Florida Keys. (Photograph © Doug Stamm)*

wiped the front section of the boat clean, to pile line in it. You don't have time to strip the nylon off the reel after you sight a fish in the water. The sun must be high. Early and late it throws shadows in the water, making a fish hard to locate.

Joe handed me a pair of glareproof sunglasses, which cut surface reflection and let the human eye penetrate into the green depths. And then they gave me my final instructions, as complicated as those a rookie gets before he goes up against a tricky hurler.

"A slow-action rod shoots line. Don't false-cast more than you have to. Drop the fly a foot or two in front of the fish; the shadow of the fly or the line across his head will flush him. Retrieve the fly slowly, in short jerks, then speed it up when the fish gets close. When he strikes, set the hook and feed the loose line through the guides with your fingers—don't allow it to foul—and then hold your rod tip high, letting him go to the end of his run against the six-pound drag. And look close. If you've never seen a bonefish, he's hard to spot at first."

Ted stepped up on the stern seat with his twelve-foot pushpole, forked on one end. Joe sat on the middle seat to instruct me and stay out of the way of any wild cast. I took the bow, an arrogant rookie with a what's-all-the-fuss-about attitude.

*An angler prepares to net a trout in Montana's scenic Armstrong Spring Creek. (Photograph © R. Valentine Atkinson)*

And I got more education in fishing that day than I've had before or since.

A shadow passed by, thirty feet off the bow of the boat. "There goes one!" I said.

Ted shook his head. "That's a barracuda. Look at his black tail. You've got to see them farther away than that."

"There's one over there to the right, then," I claimed, with a touch of triumph.

"A shark," Joe grunted. "He's too big and too black for a bonefish."

"Then what the hell does the critter look like?" I demanded.

"Maybe this will help you," Joe said. "Roughly speaking, his scientific name, Albula vulpes, means white fox. In the water he's a gray shadow, sheened over under certain conditions with a bluish or greenish cast. And he moves. A barracuda may lie motionless and a shark will cruise slowly in circles or curves. A bonefish is always going somewhere."

"There's one now!" Ted's voice crackled like a highvoltage wire. "Straight ahead of the boat, about eighty feet."

I strained my eyes until they bugged out.

"Now fifty feet," Ted snapped. "He's headed this way."

Still I saw nothing but rippling water and motionless bottom. He was thirty feet from the bateau when I finally did spot him, but by that time he'd seen us too, and turned off toward the rim of the flat that dipped into the Atlantic.

"At least," Joe said, "we know the flat's not barren today."

Twenty minutes later I got a bang as big as if I'd hit a triple when I sighted two bonefish seventy feet ahead of the boat. I'd never seen a bonefish, but I knew that's what they were. They were cutting from left to right in front of the bow.

I released the fly from my left hand and whipped a long line out toward the two fish, aiming at a point four feet in front of them, as if I were leading a slow dove in the air with a scattergun. The case was across wind, and I hadn't counted on that. The breeze caught my fly and shoved it to the water, directly over the head of the second fish. That was all. One moment I was looking at them. The next they were gone, leaving two threads of mud in their wake.

The water sizzled where Ted spat over the side of the boat. For a moment he seemed ready to bite an umpire. "Look sharp," he said, forcing a grin. "We'll see more."

Joe stood up on the seat behind me, braving the sharp barb of the Z nickel hook to furnish another pair of eyes. He spotted the next fish a hundred feet away and tried his best to point it out to me. I couldn't spot it.

*Fly fishermen cast over the ocean flats in this original painting, "A Short Cast," by artist Bob White.*

"How in the hell can you catch 'm if you can't see 'm?" Ted asked explosively.

When we reached the first point that jutted out almost to the edge of the reef, I got my first shot at a bonefish. The sun was high now and behind us, and visibility was clearer than it had been all morning. The seagoing fox cruised around the point and came directly toward us. Joe pointed him out at fifty feet and I whipped out my line for action.

This time I was a little nervous myself. I was so involved in allowing for the wind, and wondering whether my line was correctly laid out in the bottom of the boat in case I did get a strike, that I forgot to even think about my backcast. The fly was too low. It caught the brim of Ted's hat and jerked it off into the water. The fish quickened his pace and swam on into the invisible depths.

"Here," I quavered, "somebody take this pole and show me how it's done."

Ted and Joe both stubbornly shook their heads.

"You're going to catch a bonefish if we have to kick it into the boat and fasten it to your fly," Ted said.

*Class is held on the beach when you're studying fishing in sunny Miami. Shot in April 1948, this photograph captures students getting a lesson on flies and plugs. (Courtesy of the Florida State Archives)*

I was beginning to understand the jitters that come to every man on the bonefish flats. It wasn't as easy as I had planned. Not only did I fail to get the shot away, but every limestone ledge, every sand strip, began to look like a fish. Time after time I pointed—and Joe just shook his head.

"Don't worry. You'll know one when you see it."

We passed up half a dozen barracuda and at least as many sharks before I sighted another one of the white foxes. This one came from behind, on the downwind side of the boat. I saw him when I looked around to ask Joe a question and promptly forgot what I had planned to say. The fish, a big one, was boring like a torpedo through the water. I whipped out line and laid a perfect cast in front of

# FLY ROD'S NOTE BOOK

*Cornelia "Fly Rod" Crosby (1854-1946) was Maine's first licensed guide, a testament to her prowess with rifle and rod. A skilled sportswoman, Fly Rod often traveled to sporting expositions, where she promoted the sporting life of Maine, befriended sharpshooter Annie Oakley, and scandalized patrons in her short doeskin skirt. Her newspaper column detailing her hunting and fishing adventures was syndicated throughout the East.*

WHEN AT UPPER Dam last week several told me about "Augusta" catching a fish on the fly. Augusta is the sweet little nine-year-old daughter of Mr. and Mrs. Tom Miner of New York, who for several years have spent their summers in a pretty home-like camp there, and she will soon be known as the "Queen of the Pool," for it seems to be her great desire to catch a record fish and pen her name in the book of honor.

The little lady has for several years caught trout and salmon trolling with her father and as she knows the names of most of the flies he uses and can tell all about pool fishing, she asked her mother one day, "Please let me use your little fly rod?" The $50 bamboo fly rod was hanging in its place on the wall, and Mr. Miner who had been teaching her to cast the fly on the lawn took her with him out in the pool.

The little lady said, "I want a White-tipped Montreal and a Silver Doctor fly put on, Papa," and standing up in the boat, taking the rod in both her tiny hands she cast the fly out over the water. Soon there was a rise and she called, "I struck him, Papa," and he said, "Now little girlie look out for your reel, can you handle him?"

The brave little angler played the fish and reeled in a gamey pound salmon, and next at the same time had on a pair of small trout which she brought to net and asked if they could not be spared. "They are just right for breakfast, Papa," and they were cooked the next morning, and little Augusta is going to keep on trying for a 3-pounder. Here is hoping she will get him and a dainty little fly rod for the August birthday which is always celebrated.

*—Cornelia "Fly Rod" Crosby, Maine Woods, July 20, 1901*

*This "Queen of the Pool" shows off her catch in this vintage print.*

him. My heart went into my throat and stayed there while he turned toward the fly. Ted was hissing, "Strip slower—strip slower—strip slower!" I had allowed the fly to sink, and just as the fish paused behind it I gave the lure an extra twitch. He hit it in a boil of water and I set the hook.

The leader cut through the brine and the line went out while I fed it through the guides. As the fish took off for the deep I pointed my rod tip high over my head as I had been instructed to do. The last loop shooting at the guides caught around the reel handle, which was turned to the front instead of away from the jumping nylon. The rod tip jerked downward—and the line went limp: The eight-foot leader had snapped like sewing thread.

*"Saltwater King" is the title of this lively watercolor painting by artist Eldridge Hardie.*

Ted looked like he'd been caught stealing base. Joe sat down again. Nobody said a word, and my hands shook so violently that I had to pass the ragged end of the leader back to Joe and let him tie on another fly.

"Take the rod," I begged.

"You're gonna catch a fish," Ted yelled—and if they'd been listening, they could have heard him in Key Largo—"if we have to spend the winter out here." All my confidence was gone. I was as weak as if I'd run the bases ten times around, and sweating just as much. I had to produce. We went for half an hour without spotting another fish, then one slipped under the bow of the boat and flushed before I saw him. My eyes felt as though they had been out on stems a foot long for a week. Joe sat dejected on the second seat.

At last I saw a fish cruising toward us out of the shadows of the mangroves. I knew he would pass fifty or sixty feet in front of the boat.

I had to make good this time. I didn't even point him out, but dropped the fly out of my cramped fingers, looked to the handle of my reel, checked the line in the bottom of the boat, remembered to allow for the wind, and shot a cast that fell two and a half feet in front of the fish. As he turned toward it I could feel my heart bumping against my ribs. The fish slowed up and I gave the fly a short jerk—and another—

I was watching the fly when it disappeared. I set the hook and raised the rod to straighten out the line before it reached the guides. But the braided nylon did not take off to sea. It went a dizzy circle around the bateau. Ted let out a yell that echoed back from the mangroves. Joe groaned. Then I saw the bonefish turn slowly and swim away. It was seconds before I realized what had happened. A barracuda

had seen the fly and darted in ahead of the bonefish, snagging it out of his very teeth.

While I was trying to get him close enough to the beam to retrieve my hook, Ted sighted two huge bonefish lying between our boat and the island. Both were within easy casting distance. He threw his pushpole into the bateau, made a dive for the line, and almost went overboard. He caught the G-A-F on the 'cuda's next circle and with a vicious yank broke off the fly in its mouth. But the commotion had flushed the two bones out of the shallows. I reeled in line and sat down on the bow seat.

*A larger-than-life tarpon leaps near two saltwater anglers in this watercolor painting, entitled "The Contest Begins." The painter, celebrated Florida Keys artist Millard Wells, has been a member of the American Watercolor Society since 1996.*

"I hate bonefish," I said. "I wouldn't catch one if either of you were starving."

"You couldn't catch one," Ted rumbled, "if it was in a goldfish bowl. But get back up there."

"I will when somebody proves to me it can be done," I replied.

So we changed places. I went to the stern and Ted took the bow seat. Joe refused the rod.

"I'll try after you take one," he said to Ted.

Even though there is a trick to poling, I could handle the boat better than I had the bamboo, keeping the craft at an angle into the wind.

Ted's first fish was heading out to sea. The slugger made the finest cast I've ever seen for distance and accuracy, laying the line 110 feet into the stiff breeze and a foot away from the snout of the fish. The white fox saw the fly. He turned slowly, followed it for ten feet, then took it in a rush. Ted set the hook, pulled line from the floor of the boat, and let it into the guides. The end of the G-A-F shot through the tip and the squidding line followed, making the reel sing. The powerful drive of the bonefish carried him more than 700 feet against the six-pound drag on the reel before he came to the end of his run. Ted began to grind in line.

"Wouldn't it be easier," I suggested, "to strip it in?"

*A permit chases a fly in this Millard Wells painting, "Chances Are." The artist, who has yet to catch a permit on a fly, says painting this fish "is like capturing the likeness of an elusively beautiful lady in a portrait."*

Joe snorted. "He'd have it tangled in a thousand knots on his next run."

Ted dragged his fish halfway to the boat before the finny motor cranked up and ran again, pulling out the squidding line to the last turn of the spool. Twenty minutes later Ted lifted his fish gently out of the water for weighing, then released it back into the brine. On Joe's hair-trigger scales it went an even ten pounds.

Joe took over the pushpole so that Ted could show me how to shoot line into the wind and explain the necessity of using a torpedo line and a slow-action rod. He was telling me that a bonefish will flush even at the shadow of the rod across the water, so the fewer the false casts the better, when Joe pointed out another fish.

Ted cast to it, hooked and caught it—as simply as that. It looked so easy that my own ears burned when I thought of the floundering I'd done.

After Ted's second fish he handed the bamboo to Joe and went back to his pushpole. From long practice in looking beneath the surface of the water, Joe could spot a fish at distances which were remarkable to me. And he could get his shot off as accurately as Ted.

He hadn't been on the casting seat ten minutes before a bonefish tried to run us down. Joe tensed, put his weight against the line, and dropped his lure where the fish couldn't miss it. He twitched the fly twice and the bone took it in a surge that brought him toward us so fast Joe had to strip ten yards of line to set the hook. When the fish was safely on, he handed the rod toward me.

"No," I said. "I'll catch my own."

"He's a small one," Joe insisted. "A five-pounder. I only want you to know how he feels. It's the first lesson."

I took the rod. The tip was jumping like it had tied into a winner of the K. Derby. The real sang in an off-key contralto, the line hissed like a pitful of cobras. Against the six-pound drag the bone ran out four fifths of the 700-foot line. He came to a halt and I cranked in the squidding thread. I cranked until I thought my elbows would jump out of their sockets. I got him halfway in and he ran again, to the end of the skinny squidding line.

A fly reel has no hidden ratios. When you turn the handle once, the spool turns once. I got the bonefish two thirds of the way back before he made his third bid for freedom. This time it was a relief to let him go. My arms felt as though they'd been pounded with a maul.

He didn't go far on his last trip. I was a little disappointed that he didn't drag out the line to its end and give me a longer breathing spell. I wound him in and Ted lifted him out of the water.

"I know one thing," I gasped. "I'm not man enough to catch a ten-pounder, if they grow in strength as they increase in size."

"If you don't learn to throw that line," Ted grunted, "you'll never have a chance at a ten-pounder."

The sun was at its zenith. The manner in which the bright light strikes the water makes high noon the best time for fishing, but we paused long enough to gulp down the ham sandwiches Cap'n Bill and Irene had made for us.

Even when those guys ate lunch, they talked bonefish. They compared flies and decided that any good bonefish fly has white in it, that a good lure is white and brown, or white and yellow. Joe confided that his favorite has red wrappings at the head, a gray hackle, yellow body, and white wings. He tied the pattern himself and it is now manufactured commercially.

We discussed other ways of fishing for bonefish than with a fly from a slow boat. That morning we'd passed two fishermen parked on the outer edge of the reef, fishing with casting rods and shrimp—stillfishing in much the way I angled for bullheads as a boy, but on the gently rolling ocean in the sunshine.

The most fascinating way to fish for bonefish is to wade along the flats at low tide, when the water is knee deep. In this way, as from a boat, the fish may be spotted either when they cruise along, watching for small minnows to dart out of the ragged bottom growth, or when they are tailing, with their heads in the rocks and grass, rooting out crabs and worms. Feeding in the sandy or muddy stretches, they throw up a cloud in the water. These "muds" indicate fish as definitely as his tail above the water, flashing silver in the sun.

When a man wades he's on his own, with no other eyes, no other hands, to help him. Then bonefishing takes on the aspects of big-game hunting, where you must find your quarry, approach cautiously to keep from spooking it, and make a perfect shot. In bonefishing, though, the shot is just the beginning of the fun.

"You don't see as many fish when you wade," Ted explained.

One thing that appealed to me is that when you go bonefishing you can spend as much or as little as you want. You can park your car along the edge of one of the many flats and wade out from shore. You can rent a bateau and a motor at almost any fishing camp, or you can pay up to sixty dollars a day for expert guides and services to insure your luck. Joe estimates that there are some 500 square miles of bonefish flats around the Florida Keyes, and they're never crowded, though sometimes sixty fish a day are entered in the Metropolitan Miami Fishing Tournament. Best seasons of the year on the flats are from April through July and September through December.

Ted was casting an anxious eye at the sun, which still clung to high noon.

"Let's go—let's go," he said impatiently. "It'll be sundown and this game'll be called on account of darkness."

I took the bow again, laying out my line on the deck. I had learned to distinguish the black tail of the 'cuda from the dark, sinuous form of a shark. But the wind was blowing a little harder now, wrinkling the water's surface and making the fish more difficult to see. I felt like a guy standing at home plate with two outs, two strikes, and the bases loaded. If I fanned again I'd probably find myself on the bench for the remainder of the season.

Joe pointed to a couple of muds. "Looks hot in there," he said.

But by the time I had seen where the fish were mudding, they had slipped out from under the screen and were gone.

One nice bone came from behind and plowed beyond the longest cast before we saw him. And then I spotted one headed directly to the boat. Quickly I checked my stance and the lay of the line, estimated how far I'd have to lead him—allowing for the wind—and shot a fly that fell exactly in place. I didn't even have a chance to strip it in. The bonefish hit it with a thrust as savage as a peg to second and I hardly had time to drop the smoking line from my fingers. I cleared the screaming nylon through the guides and held the rod tip up. When the reel began to sing, Joe's sigh of relief was audible.

*Dusk falls around a solitary angler plying the slow, clear waters of Millionaire's Pool in Henry's Fork. (Photograph © R. Valentine Atkinson)*

"He's a big one," Ted sang, "a big one! Boy, you sure hit that one on the nose!"

"Maybe he's a world record," Joe opined.

The line didn't even slow down. It smoked through the guides to the end of the backing and came to an abrupt and violent halt at the knot fastening it around the spool. The bamboo bucked in my hands and the line went limp. His last surging drive had carried the big fish far enough to break the eight-pound-test leader. I reeled in slowly, sick all the way to my toes. That had been in big fish. I'd hooked him fair and square, going through all the intricate process to—another error.

Joe's face was a mixture of disappointment that I'd fanned my big chance and relief that his bat in my hands was still intact. Ted made the kindest comment he could under the circumstances.

"Oh well," he said, "no man bats a thousand in the bonefish league."

CHAPTER TWO

# Fly Fishing Country

"I SALUTE THE GALLANTRY AND UNCOMPROMISING STANDARDS OF WILD TROUT, AND THEIR TASTES IN LANDSCAPES."

–*John Madson, Up on the River*

# A Quiet Week

(with apologies to Garrison Keillor)

By John Gierach

John Gierach needs little introduction to fly fishing readers. The acclaimed author of *Where the Trout Are All As Long As Your Leg* (1991), *Even Brook Trout Get the Blues* (1992), *Another Lousy Day in Paradise* (1996), *Standing in a River Waving a Stick* (1999), and several other essay collections, Gierach is the sport's premier humorist.

From his home on the St. Vrain River in Colorado, Gierach writes about the pleasures and pains of fly fishing with his characteristic ironic tone. His columns appear regularly in *Fly Rod & Reel*, *Sports Afield*, and the Longmont, Colorado, *Daily Times-Call*. Also an artist, Gierach has illustrated several of his works with line drawings.

This story is taken from Gierach's 1990 book, *Sex, Death, and Fly-Fishing*. In it, Lake Wobegon meets Colorado fly fishing country as Gierach, a Midwesterner by birth, borrows the gentle ironic musings of another famous Midwestern satirist.

PREVIOUS PAGE, MAIN IMAGE: *Tumbling fifty feet over a green hillside, the glorious waters of the Sacramento River's Mossbrae Falls serve as a mystical backdrop to fly fishing. (Photograph © R. Valentine Atkinson)*

PREVIOUS PAGE, INSET IMAGE: *An angler drops his fly line in Wisconsin's craggy Apple River Falls in this 1905 picture by professional Minneapolis photographer Louis D. Sweet. (Courtesy of the Minnesota Historical Society)*

LEFT: *Storm clouds approach an angler fishing Armstrong Spring Creek. (Photograph © R. Valentine Atkinson)*

IT HAS BEEN a quiet week in East Big Fish. Lance, the owner of the Pompous Angler Fly Shop, was over at the Cafe Eat the other morning with his wife, Muffy. They were having dry whole wheat toast and herbal tea, as usual, and Lance seemed to be in sort of a poor mood. He even got a little short with Agnes when she kidded him about how maybe he wouldn't be as sour in the mornings if he started eating a man's breakfast like the rest of the boys.

Agnes really was kidding, too. I mean, she started serving that herbal tea because Lance and Muffy, and some of their customers, had asked for it in the first place. If Lance had said what he'd said ("Why don't you mind your own business?") with one eye closed and a half smile on his face as others at the Cafe Eat do, it would have been okay. But he didn't.

When Agnes brought their tea, you could hear the saucers hit the table from out in the parking lot.

Lance was depressed because, as he'd mentioned the day before, and the day before that, the out-of-state fishermen were going to other rivers—and, presumably, other fly shops—because the hatches there were on time, while here the *Ephemerella infrequens* had come off before the season even opened and now the *Ephemerella doddsi* were late.

*Bison and anglers warily go about their separate business in Yellowstone National Park's Mud Volcano Thermal Area. (Photograph © Jeff Henry/Roche Jaune Pictures, Inc.)*

I overheard that from a nearby table where I was sitting with Harvey, of Harvey's Gas Worms Cold Beer Groceries and Fishing Tackle. He leaned over and said to me, in an informative tone, "I think he's referring to the fact that the fish ain't been biting lately." Harvey has been in the tackle business for forty-three years and likes to help clear things up when the talk gets overly technical.

We're a trout fishing town here, all 427 year-around residents, so cafe discussions of how the fishing has been are a little more serious than they are in some other places. When Harvey finally told Agnes what Lance was upset about, she forgave him—she hadn't realized it was so serious—although she continues to insist that a few cups of regular old hot coffee in the morning would do his disposition a world of good.

Directly or indirectly, just about everything here depends on the fishing. There's the K.O.A. Campground and the Brown Trout Guest Cabins north of town and, in the downtown business loop itself, there's Harvey's Gas Worms, etc., the relatively new Pompous Angler, and the much older Bob's Flies and Guide Service, not to mention the town's two dining establishments, the Cafe Eat and the Roundup Cafe, plus the Branding Iron Bar and the Suds-N-Duds Laundromat. All of these places have stuffed trout on their walls (even the Laundromat) and are patronized heavily by fishermen in season (even the Laundromat) and probably wouldn't survive otherwise.

*Fly fishermen scout their waterway in search of elusive trout. (Photograph © R. Valentine Atkinson)*

If you don't own or work in one of these places, guide, or tie flies, you either get bused into the county seat to school or just hang around home all day. Whatever you do, you know what everyone else does and you know how the fishing has been lately.

It's a typical small town in that if you were born here or are only here for a week of fishing, you're welcome. But if you move here from somewhere else you're viewed with considerable suspicion.

Lance and Muffy found that out when they opened the new fly shop which, being of the Swiss chalet persuasion, stands out on Main Street like a flying saucer and made a lot of people uneasy at first. Not the least of them was Bob, who said publicly that any idiot could see there was only enough business for one fly shop and there was already one here. And, he added, it had been here for two generations. As any resident of any small tourist community knows, the scale of time that really counts is measured in generations. Everything else is just dust in the wind.

Harvey was neutral, since he also sells food and gas and his fishing tackle consists largely of salmon eggs, garlic-flavored marshmallows, and worms.

Through that first fishing season, Bob would not actually speak to Lance,

*A fly-caught rainbow trout. (Photograph © Erwin and Peggy Bauer)*

although when he ran into him he'd nod and grunt in the interest of civility. But then it began to look like there was enough business to go around.

For one thing, the locals who didn't use worms went to Bob's because they'd always gone there, even back when Bob himself was in high school and guiding for his dad in the summers. And most of the old customers—after a quick stop at the Pompous Angler just to look around—came back, too. Fishermen are a fickle bunch, but once they hit middle age they do seem to develop some loyalties. Either that, or they're just too stubborn and set in their ways to change.

After a while we began to notice a distinct difference between the clientele of the two shops: Bob got the older guys driving American pickups and wearing canvas chest waders and floppy hats. And no women to speak of. Lance's customers were some younger, drove cars (often foreign), and wore skintight neoprene waders and caps. Many were accompanied by wives or lady friends dressed pretty much the same way.

Eventually it got to where we could sit around the cafe and tell who was shopping at which fly store. Aside from their general appearance, Lance's customers asked about the "no smoking" section (there isn't one) and talked earnestly about hatches and spinner falls using lots of Latin terminology. A lot of the guys from Bob's smoked pipes and spoke more casually of Royal Wulffs and Hares Ears. And anyway, many of the latter looked familiar, that is, if not the individuals, then at least the type.

Agnes—who had begun to sell the hell out of herbal tea and bran muffins—was one of the early peacemakers, urging Bob to "live and let live" in the fly shop department. And Bob did, finally.

It happened in the second season after Lance arrived. A couple of young guys from New York came in and asked if the *Ptaronarcys californicus* had begun to emerge yet and, although Bob could easily have translated that into black stone fly, he said, "Maybe you ought to go ask Lance about that."

It turned out to be a good move all around. The guys bought their licenses and flies from Lance, but then came back to Bob's saying, "His guides were all booked, but he said you had some funky old wooden mack boats and good local guides."

Funky? Bob thought.

Lance's boats are bright yellow, fiberglass, and up until that moment Bob had been a little jealous. In fact, one night at the Branding Iron, right after the Pompous Angler opened, Bob had a few too many beers and admitted to feeling a little old and worn out lately, pointing out that he was fifty-two and no kid anymore, and couldn't afford a whole fleet of new boats like "some people."

But the two guys from New York seemed to kind of turn him around on that. He guided them himself because all his regular guides were already out. They caught lots of big trout, some on the entomologically correct *Pteronarcys* nymphs Lance had sold them, but most on Bob's Black Uglies, which are a local variation of the Wooly Worm.

*"When I first started fly-fishing it was largely because of the idea of casting, that incredible suspension of the line overhead, the sweeping curve following, in a delayed reaction, the motion of the rod."—Wayne Fields,* What the River Knows, *1990 (Photograph © Jeff Henry/Roche Jaune Pictures, Inc.)*

Later the two sports bragged about the neat old guide they'd found with a few missing teeth, a slow, casual pace, and corny good humor who got them into more trout than they'd seen before in their collective lifetimes. They'd called him "Sir" for a while until Bob told them to cut it out.

After that Bob took to wearing his cowboy hat again and began doing more trips himself. He lost a little weight, too, and got a nice tan. He never talked about it, but if I had to guess I'd say he stopped feeling old and started feeling venerable; a fine distinction, but an important one. Young people calling you "Sir" can do that.

And, for that matter, after a couple of seasons Lance's chamois shirts faded, lost their nap, and got threadbare at the elbows—from rowing, some said, while others claimed it was from leaning on the counter. His beard went gradually from professorial to just country, and he started stocking Bob's Uglies in the shop.

Then, just last summer, a famous fishing writer came to town and drove straight to Lance's shop where he parked his Land Rover under the big molded plastic mayfly sign that said OPEN. After carefully writing down all the best hatches and all the best times of year to fish, he asked about the history of the river, and Lance said, "Bob's the one who can tell you about that. He was born here."

Lance walked the writer the two blocks over to Bob's shop and introduced him in such a way that if Bob had never heard of the guy, he'd at least understand that he should have. The three of them ended up having lunch together at the Cafe Eat (the meat loaf special) and then they all went fishing. Bob and Lance took the writer to the best spots, got him into lots of trout, and sent him home with fifteen rolls of exposed film, pages of notes, and stars in his eyes. Then Bob and Lance went and had a drink together.

Bob said, "Shoot, that guy could hardly fish, and you say he's famous?"

"He is famous," Lance said.

"Well," Bob replied, "you're a better fisherman than he is." That was a left-handed compliment, but it was the best Bob could do. Lance figured it was good enough.

It took the better part of five years, but Lance and Muffy are now widely considered to be residents, although only their children will be seen as legitimate East

*Painter Eldridge Hardie suffuses this original oil painting, "Wyoming September," with golden hues that capture the beauty of an autumn day. Hardie, who has made a career as a wildlife artist, says of his work: "I was born to hunt, fish, and make art about these passions."*

Big Fishers. It helped a lot that they spend the winters here. If you don't spend the winters here, you are from wherever you *do* spend them.

The feud which, looking back on it now, didn't really amount to much, probably helped, too. Making peace with someone tends to bring them into the fold, but before you can make peace, you have to have a little war. The other day when Muffy came into the cafe complaining about a couple of idiot tourists, everyone sympathized without a trace of irony.

"I wish they'd just go back where they came from," Muffy said, and Bob replied from a neighboring table, "That's the nice part about it, honey. Sooner or later they all do."

Muffy has pretty much stopped bristling at being called "Honey."

The river flows under the two-lane bridge down at the end of Main Street. It's a decent trout river for its size; not the best in the state, but not too many notches down from the top either. You'll read about it now and then in what Lance calls "the literature." It's pretty slow through here with some long riffles—nothing you could call rapids even at high water—and lots of good, braided dry fly water. It's plenty big enough to float, but small enough to wade, too, and you can fish it nicely either way.

And it's a beautiful river, even to those of us who have seen it every day of our lives, and so don't even really look at the thing for weeks on end.

There are some fine hatches, but it can be moody, which is why most of us locals, following Bob's lead, fish it with nymphs. You can almost always get 'em on nymphs. We tend to find a hole and fish the hell out of it while the drift boats shoot past. Sometimes the fancy sports look down their noses at us as if we didn't really belong here, even though it is, of course, the other way around.

Lance, on the other hand, is a dry fly fisherman. He carries five times the number of flies any of us do and covers that much more water in a day's fishing. He's a pretty caster to watch and even Bob allows as how the guy can catch a lot of fish.

If you asked anyone on the street, they'd tell you that Lance catches more trout, but Bob catches more *big* trout; and also that Bob does best in higher water, while Lance really comes into his own in the lower flows of late summer and fall. It's a kind of natural division of labor with a changing of the guard sometime in late July or early August.

The tourist fishermen begin to arrive about the time the river comes down from the spring runoff and the early hatches start. Some are wide-eyed and excited—mostly the young ones who have read about our river here in magazines and books and have finally made the pilgrimage. The older guys tend to be a little slower and more businesslike, but they're excited, too, having learned on many past vacations just how good the river can be if you have the patience to wait it out.

*Anglers crowd a popular stretch of Yellowstone River near Cascade Lake Picnic Area. (Photograph © Jeff Henry/Roche Jaune Pictures, Inc.)*

*A full fly box and a trusty rod and reel are essentials for a day on the river. (Photograph © R. Valentine Atkinson)*

The old hands know that Bob's guides are the ones to hire early in the season because they're a bit older, live here year around, and have had the chance to scope the water out before the season started. Lance's guides are college kids who have only been in town for a week before their first trips. Even the local kids haven't really checked out the river; they've been too busy looking up old sweethearts and boozing it up with old pals. They are young, strong, enthusiastic, and good boatmen. They're the best to hire later in the season when things get hot and heavy.

By the middle of summer the town is packed with fly-fishermen. Most live in campers or tents, either at the K.O.A. or at one of the Forest Service campgrounds, but the Brown Trout Guest Cabins are full all summer long, too. Both cafés serve fishermen's specials and, although the Suds-N-Duds isn't exactly crowded, it gets used. Sam, the owner, says the dryers see more action than the washing machines.

We're a few miles off the main highway here, so there's hardly any traffic except for mornings and evenings, and then you see cars with license plates from all over the country and pickup trucks towing mack boats to put-in and take-out points along the river.

Harvey's Gas Worms Cold Beer Groceries and Fishing Tackle always does a good business, although Harvey himself tends to deny it. I mean, everyone either staying in town or passing through needs or wants at least one of the aforementioned items, and since Harvey's is the only store worthy of the name for sixteen miles in one direction and thirty-one in the other, he can charge pretty much what he wants—which is a lot.

Harvey also sells a lot of worms, so many that the van from Merl's Worm Ranch shows up twice a week to fill the cooler with fresh ones. Some think that's odd, since the river right through here is catch-and-release, flies only now. But Harvey knows there are lots of other places to fish, like the reservoir, some lakes, and a couple of small streams, where people can use bait and kill fish like the Good Lord intended. Harvey has nothing against fly-fishermen, although he thinks some of them are way too serious about it, but he does have something against catch-and-release regulations.

"It just ain't natural," he sometimes observes.

Harvey is something of an expert on worms, although no one around here can remember the last time he actually went fishing. You tell him where you're going, and he'll recommend red worms, crawlers, or Georgia jumpers.

Lance naturally thinks the no-kill rule is great and wouldn't have started his shop here without it.

It's Bob who's neutral on this one. He knows it's good for business in at least two ways: it keeps fish in the river (and Bob knows that a river can get fished out, he's seen it happen) and it also attracts a certain class of fishermen, namely guys who are willing to spend money and who don't choke at $1.50 for a dry fly.

Still, he remembers the days when catch-and-release regulations weren't *necessary* and sort of misses them. He misses the fish fries out on the sandbars in the evenings, and the guys who used to come in to show him a big, dripping stringer of trout they'd killed using his nymphs. A few times a year someone would come in with a real pig, and ask about a taxidermist.

The most recent mount on his wall is a lovely, fat, four-pound brook trout that was killed in a nearby pond, but most of the others came from the river. The biggest, a sixteen-pound, four-ounce brown, was taken in 1957. It's a pretty mount, but it's beginning to look a little ratty, and the guy who caught the fish is dead. Bob sometimes looks at it and thinks, Anyone can have a hog trout from thirty years ago.

But from his newfound vantage point as the gray-haired, fly-fishing sage of East Big Fish, he is philosophical. "Well," he says, "things change."

Things do change. The fishing is still as good as it ever was, but it's harder now and it seems as if there are more fly-fishermen every season. Most of us who actually live here don't fish the river much until late in the year when the weather gets unpredictable and the crowd thins out some. We fish the lakes and streams and do pretty well for ourselves, though. It would be nice to be able to get on the river more, and we sometimes complain about it, but we know that without all these people around here for four or five months out of the year, the place would probably dry up and blow away.

I guess we have one of those love/hate things with the tourists, but, whatever else they're like, they're on a fishing trip and they're happy. It's hard to hold that against anyone.

I guess what I'm trying to say is, we mostly love 'em more than we hate 'em.

Speaking of tourists, Harvey started renting videotapes this year. He did that at the insistence of his wife, Ethel, who said it was something city people expected now. So above the weathered wooden sign proclaiming Gas Worms Cold Beer Groceries and Fishing Tackle, they added a red-and-yellow plastic one that flashes off and on and says VIDEO MANIA PIT STOP. They even tumbled for a small adult section (something else city people expect), and one night, after reading the titles and looking at the covers, they decided to take a VCR home and watch a few, just to make sure they weren't too awful to have in the store.

Ten minutes into the first one, Ethel said to Harvey, "You can watch this foolishness of you want to. I'm going to bed." Which she did, taking more time at it and making more noise than usual.

When she got up at six the next morning, Harvey was still in front of the TV watching Leather Hospital in which these two young nurses were . . . Well, never mind.

She said she was ashamed of him, but she wasn't. I mean, you keep your mouth shut about the things you're really ashamed of, and Ethel ended up telling everyone in town and half her customers about it over the next week. It came out as a complaint, but I thought she was actually proud of Harvey for still being that frisky at his age. When I mentioned that to her one day, she came dangerously close to smiling and said, "Well, at least he didn't take the VCR apart to see how it worked."

Whenever this came up Harvey would always quickly change the subject by saying, "Sure, I looked at a couple of them, but mostly I was watching those Masters Series tapes on fly-fishing. The trout are bitin' now, by the way. The *Ephemerella doddsi* hatch was late this year, but they started coming off just the other day. It's been real good."

And it *has* been good. The first day the bugs came off there was almost no one in town and me and some of the boys had the Bend Pool and most of the meadow stretch all to ourselves. Trout were rising everywhere, so we fished dry flies. And yes, we already had some in our boxes. We're not hicks, you know.

Now, after only two or three days, the word has spread and every guide in town is working. There seem to be more strange faces than usual rowing the boats this year.

*A handsome fly box packed with an assortment of flies is one of an angler's prize possessions. (Photograph © Howard Lambert)*

Many of the guides are still college kids, but fewer and fewer of them are from here. A lot of our kids go off to college now swearing they'll never come back and, sure enough, don't, except for the odd Christmas or family funeral. We hear how their lives are going, but we don't really know what *happens* to them the way we'd know if they stayed around here.

Oh, sure, we know in a general way that they get caught up in another kind of life. Hell, some of them get caught up in that while they're still here, which accounts for, among other things, the occasional tart whiff of marijuana you'll sometimes walk into on Main Street on a warm summer evening. We know it's the kind of life you eventually have to get away from by going someplace—like here, for instance—to fly-fish for trout for a few weeks. The kind of life where "How's the fishing?" is considered to be idle chatter.

# *Colorado Trails*

*By Zane Grey*

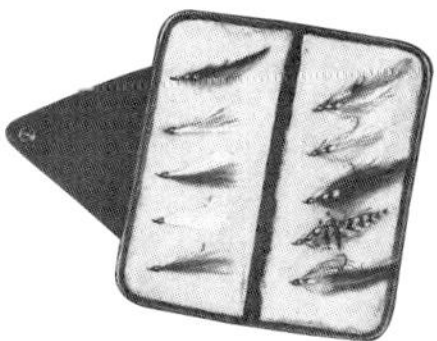

Pearl Zane Gray (1872–1939) is the classic self-made man. Aiming for distinction, he shed his first name and changed the spelling of his last name—then abandoned a respectable career in dentistry to live the adventure of the Wild West. And he wrote about it, amassing a mile-long list of bestsellers and a fortune that allowed him to explore the world.

As grandfather of the Western novel, Grey authored nearly one hundred chart-topping books, including the enduring *Riders of the Purple Sage* (1912). He sold his stories to "pulp" magazines and a slew of outdoors publications such as *Field & Stream*, *Country Gentleman*, and *Izaak Walton Monthly*.

Here, Grey waxes poetic on the wild, lonely beauty of his beloved West, then launches into classic adventure mode with the ongoing saga of his piscatorial rivalry with brother R. C., who appears in countless stories over the years. *Outdoor Life* first printed this article in its March–June 1918 issue.

LEFT: *A fully equipped fly fisherman fights a trout in Montana's Big Hole River. (Photograph © R. Valentine Atkinson)*

RIDING AND TRAMPING trails would lose half their charm if the motive were only to hunt and to fish. It seems fair to warn the reader who longs to embark upon a bloody game hunt or a chronicle of fishing records that this is not that kind of story. But it will be one for those who love horses and dogs, the long winding dim trails, the wild flowers and the dark still woods, the fragrance of spruce and the smell of camp fire smoke. And as well for those who love to angle in brown lakes or rushing brooks or chase after the baying hounds or stalk the stag on his lonely heights.

We left Denver on August 22nd over the Moffet road and had a long wonderful ride through the mountains. The Rockies have a sweep, a limitless sweep, majestic and grand. For many miles we crossed no streams, and climbed and wound up barren slopes. Once across the divide, however, we descended into a country of black forests and green valleys. Yampa, a little hamlet with a past prosperity, lay in the wide valley of the Bear River. It was picturesque but idle, and a better name for it would have been Sleepy Hollow. The main and only street was very wide and dusty, bordered by old boardwalks and vacant stores. It seemed a deserted street of a deserted village. Teague, the guide, lived there. He assured me it was not quite as lively a place as in the early days when it was a stage center for an old and rich mining section. We stayed there at the one hotel for a whole day, most of which I spent sitting on the boardwalk. Whenever I chanced to look down the wide street it seemed always the same—deserted. But Yampa had the charm of being old and forgotten, and for that reason I would like to live there a while.

On August 23rd we started in two buckboards for the foothills, some fifteen miles westward, where Teague's men were to meet us with saddle and pack horses. We arrived at the edge of the foothills about noon. It appeared to be the gateway of a valley, with aspen groves and ragged jack-pines on the slopes, and a stream running down. Our driver called it the Stillwater. That struck me as strange, for the stream was in a great hurry. R. C. spied trout in it, and schools of darkish, mullet-like fish which we were informed were grayling. We wished for our tackle then and for time to fish.

Teague's man, a young fellow called Virgil, met us here. He did not resemble the ancient Virgil in the least, but he did look as if he had

*An angler gazes upon wild McCloud River winding through a California wood. (Photograph © R. Valentine Atkinson)*

walked right out of one of my romances of wild riders. So I took a liking to him at once.

But the bunch of horses he had corralled there did not excite any delight in me. Horses, of course, were the most important part of our outfit. And that moment of first seeing the horses that were to carry us on such long rides was an anxious and thrilling one. I have felt it many times, and it never grows any weaker from experience. Many a scrubby lot of horses had turned out well upon acquaintance, and some I had found hard to part with at the end of trips. Up to that time, however, I had not seen a bear hunter's horses; and I was much concerned by the fact that these were a sorry looking outfit, dusty, ragged, maneless, cut and bruised and crippled. Still, I reflected, they were bunched up so closely that I could not tell much about them, and I decided to wait for Teague before I chose a horse for anyone.

*American artist Adolf Dehn (1895-1968) created this delicate lithograph, "Trout Fishing on the Gunnison," in 1941. Born in rural Minnesota, Dehn moved on to art circles in Europe and New York but never lost his passion for the natural world. (Courtesy of the Minnesota Historical Society)*

In an hour Teague trotted up to our resting place. Beside his own mount he had two white saddle horses, and nine pack animals, heavily laden. Teague was a sturdy rugged man with bronzed face and keen gray-blue eyes, very genial and humorous. Straightway I got the impression that he liked work.

"Let's organize," he said, briskly. "Have you picked the horses you're goin' to ride?"

Teague led from the midst of that dusty kicking bunch a rangy powerful horse, with four white feet, a white face and a noble head. He had escaped my eye. I felt that here at least was one horse.

The rest of the horses were permanently crippled or temporarily lame, and I had no choice, except to take the one it would be kindest to ride.

"He ain't much like your Silvermane or Black Star," said Teague, laughing.

"What do you know about them?" I asked, very much pleased.

"Well, I know all about them," he replied. "I'll have you the best horse in this country in a few days. Fact is I've bought him an' he'll come with my cowboy, Vern. . . . Now, we're organized. Let's move."

We rode through a meadow along a spruce slope above which towered the great mountain. It was a zigzag trail, rough, boggy, and steep in places. The Stillwater meandered here, and little breaks on the water gave evidence of feeding trout. We had several miles of meadow, and then sheered off to the left up into the timber. It was a spruce forest, very still and fragrant. We climbed out up on a bench, and across a flat, up another bench, out of the timber into the patches of snow. Here snow could be felt in the air. Water was everywhere. I saw a fox, a badger, and another furry creature, too illusive to name. One more climb brought us to the top of the Flattop Pass, about eleven thousand feet. The view in the direction from which we had come was splendid, and led the eye to the distant sweeping ranges, dark and dim along the horizon. The Flattops were flat enough, but not very wide at this pass, and we were soon going down again into a green gulf of spruce, with ragged peaks lifting beyond. Here again I got the suggestion of limitless space. It took us an hour to ride down to Little Trappers Lake, a small clear green sheet of water. The larger lake was farther down. It was big, irregular, and bordered by spruce forests, and shadowed by the lofty gray peaks.

The camp was on the far side. The air appeared rather warm, and mosquitoes bothered us. However, they did not stay long. It was after sunset and I was too tired to have many impressions.

Our cook appeared to be a melancholy man. He had a deep quavering voice, a long drooping mustache and sad eyes. He was silent most of the time. The men called him Bill, and yelled when they spoke, for he was somewhat deaf. It did not take me long to discover that he was a good cook.

Our tent was pitched down the slope from the cook tent. We were too tired to sit round a camp fire and talk. The stars were white and splendid, and they hung over the flat ridges like great beacon lights. The lake appeared to be inclosed on three sides by amphitheatric mountains, black with spruce up to the gray walls of rock. The night grew cold and very still. The bells on the horses tinkled distantly. There was a soft murmur of falling water. A lonesome coyote barked, and that thrilled me. Teague's dogs answered this prowler, and some of them had voices to make a hunter thrill. One, the bloodhound Cain, had a roar like a lion's. I had not gotten acquainted with the hounds, and I was thinking about them when I fell asleep.

Next morning I was up at five-thirty. The air was cold and nipping and frost shone on grass and sage. A red glow of sunrise gleamed on the tip of the mountain and slowly grew downward.

The cool handle of an axe felt good. I soon found, however, that I could not wield it long for lack of breath. The elevation was close to ten thousand feet and the air at that height was thin and rare. After each series of lusty strokes I had to rest. R. C., who could handle an axe as he used to swing a baseball bat, made fun of my efforts. Whereupon I relinquished the tool to him, and chuckled at his discomfort.

After breakfast R. C. and I got out tackles and rigged up fly rods, and sallied forth to the lake with the same eagerness we had felt when we were boys after chubs and sunfish. The lake glistened green in the sunlight and it lay like a gem at the foot of the magnificent black slopes.

The water was full of little floating particles that Teague called wild rice. I thought the lake had begun to work, like eastern lakes during dog days. It did not look propitious for fishing, but Teague reassured us. The outlet of this lake was the head of White River. We tried the outlet first, but trout were not rising there. Then we began wading and casting along a shallow bar of the lake. Teague had instructed us to cast, then drag the flies slowly across the surface of the water, in imitation of a swimming fly or bug. I tried this, and several times, when the leader was close to me and my rod far back, I had strikes. With my rod in that position I could not hook the trout. Then I cast my own way, letting the flies sink a little. To my surprise and dismay I had only a few strikes and could not hook the fish.

R. C., however, had better luck, and that, too, in wading right over the ground I had covered. To beat me at anything always gave him the most unaccountable pleasure.

"These are educated trout," he said. "It takes a skillful fisherman to make them rise. Now anybody can catch the big game of the sea, which is your forte. But here you are N. G. . . . Watch me cast!"

*Steam rises from the Snake River in Teton National Park. (Photograph © Dennis Frates)*

I watched him make a most atrocious cast with his double flying. But the water boiled, and he hooked two good-sized trout at once. Quite speechless with envy and admiration I watched him play them and eventually beach them. They were cutthroat trout, silvery-sided and marked with the red slash along their gills that gave them their name. I did not catch any while wading, but from the bank I spied one, and dropping a fly in front of his nose, I got him. R. C. caught four more, all about a pound in weight, and then he had a strike that broke his leader. He did not have another leader, so we walked back to camp.

Wild flowers colored the open slopes leading down out of the forest. Goldenrod, golden daisies, and bluebells were plentiful and very pretty. Here I found my first columbine, the beautiful flower that is the emblem of Colorado. In vivid contrast to its blue, Indian paintbrush thinly dotted the slopes and varied in color from red to pink and from white to yellow.

My favorite of all wild flowers—the purple asters—were there too, on tall nodding stems, with pale faces held up to the light. The reflection of mountain and forest in Trappers Lake was clear and beautiful.

*"Sportsman's Paradise": A fly fisherman nets his catch in this idyllic scene.*

In the afternoon R. C. and I went out again to try for trout. I found a place between two willow banks at the lake's outlet where trout were breaking on the surface. It took a long cast for me, but about every tenth attempt I would get a fly over the right place and raise a fish. They were small, but that did not detract from my gratification. The light on the water was just right for me to see the trout rise, and that was a beautiful sight as well as a distinct advantage. I had caught four small fish when a shout from R. C. called me quickly downstream. I found him standing in the middle of a swift chute with his rod bent double and a long line out.

"Got a whale!" he yelled. "See him—down there—in that white water. See him flash red! . . . Go down there and land him for me. Hurry! He's got all the line!"

I ran below to an open place in the willows. Here the stream was shallow and very swift. In the white water I caught a flashing gleam of red. Then I saw the shine of the leader. But I could not reach it without wading in. When I did this the trout lunged out. He looked crimson and silver. I could have put my fist in his mouth.

"Grab the leader! Yank him out!" yelled R. C. in desperation. "There! He's got all the line."

"But it'd be better to wade down," I yelled back.

He shouted that the water was too deep and for me to save his fish. This was an awful predicament for me. I knew the instant I grasped the leader that the big trout would break it or pull free. The same situation, with different kinds of fish, had presented itself many times on my numberless fishing jaunts with R. C. and they all crowded to my mind. Nevertheless I had no choice. Plunging in to my knees I frantically reached for the leader. The red trout made a surge. I missed him. R. C. yelled that something would break. That was no news to me. Another plunge brought me in touch with the leader. Then I essayed to lead the huge cutthroat ashore. He was heavy. But he was tired and that provided hope. Near the shore as I was about to lift him, he woke up, swam round me twice, then ran between my legs.

*A beautiful rainbow trout glides through crystal clear waters. (Photograph © R. Valentine Atkinson)*

When, a little later, R. C. came panting downstream I was sitting on the bank, all wet, with one knee skinned, and I was holding his broken leader in my hands. Strange to say, he went into a rage! Blamed me for the loss of that big trout! Under such circumstances it was always best to maintain silence and I did so as long as I could. After his paroxysm had spent itself and he had become somewhat near a rational being once more, he asked me:

"Was he big?"

"Oh—a whale of a trout!" I replied.

"Humph! Well, how big?"

Thereupon I enlarged upon the exceeding size and beauty of that trout. I made him out very much bigger than he actually looked to me and I minutely described his beauty and wonderful gaping mouth. R. C. groaned and that was my revenge.

The next day, September 1st, we rode down along the outlet of Big Fish to White River and down that for miles to fish for grayling. The stream was large and swift and cold. It appeared full of ice water and rocks, but no fish. We met fishermen, an automobile, and a camp outfit. That was enough for me. Where an automobile can run, I do not belong. The fishing was poor. But the beautiful open valley, flowered in gold and purple, was recompense for a good deal of bad luck.

# *Fishing the Rhone Canal*

Ernest Hemingway

Ernest Miller Hemingway (1899–1961) not only transformed the style of American prose, he brought the angler's experience to the highest pinnacle of literary tradition. From Nick Adams in "Big Two-Hearted River" (1924) to Jake Barnes in *The Sun Also Rises* (1926), Hemingway's war-bitten heroes find solace in a swift, cold trout stream.

As a cub reporter for the Kansas City *Star* and a European correspondent for the Toronto *Star*, Hemingway developed his lean, journalist style. He wrote such classics as *A Farewell to Arms* (1929), *For Whom the Bell Tolls* (1940), and the Pulitzer Prize-winning *The Old Man and the Sea* (1952). In 1954, he was awarded the Nobel Prize for Literature.

This article first appeared in the Toronto *Daily Star* on June 10, 1922. In it, we witness a young writer practice a theme he would perfect: the regenerative effect of fishing on a war-wounded spirit.

LEFT: *A cutthroat trout leaps upstream to spawn. (Photograph © Jeff Henry/Roche Jaune Pictures, Inc.)*

GENEVA, SWITZERLAND.—In the afternoon a breeze blows up the Rhone valley from Lake Geneva. Then you fish up-stream with the breeze at your back, the sun on the back of your neck, the tall white mountains on both sides of the green valley and the fly dropping very fine and far off on the surface and under the edge of the banks of the little stream, called the Rhone canal, that is barely a yard wide, and flows swift and still.

Once I caught a trout that way. He must have been surprised at the strange fly and he probably struck from bravado, but the hook set and he jumped into the air twice and zigged nobly back and forth toward every patch of weed at the current bottom until I slid him up the side of the bank.

He was such a fine trout that I had to keep unwrapping him to take a look and finally the day got so hot that I sat under a pine tree on the back of the stream and unwrapped the trout entirely and ate a paper-bag full of cherries I had and read the trout-dampened Daily Mail. It was a hot day, but I could look out across the green, slow valley past the line of trees that marked the course of the Rhone and watch a waterfall coming down the brown face of the mountain. The fall came out of a glacier that reached down toward a little town with four grey houses and three grey churches that was planted on the side of the mountain and looked solid, the waterfall, that is, until you saw it was moving. Then it looked cool and flickering, and I wondered who lived in the four houses and who went to the three churches with the sharp stone spires.

*Anglers nap during fly fishing's midday lull. (Photograph © R. Valentine Atkinson)*

Now if you wait until the sun gets down behind the big shoulder of the Savoie Alps where France joins on to Switzerland, the wind changes in the Rhone valley and a cool breeze comes down from the mountains and blows down stream toward the Lake of Geneva. When this breeze comes and the sun is going down, great shadows come out from the mountains, the cows with their manypitched bells begin to be driven along the road, and you fish down the stream.

There are a few flies over the water and every little while some big trout rises and goes "plop" where a tree hangs over the water. You can hear the "plop" and look back of you up the stream and see the circles on the water where the fish jumped. Then is the time to rewrap the trout in Lord Northcliff's latest speech reported verbatim, the reported imminent demise of the coalition, the thrilling story

*This vintage poster advertises London's historic express railway, the luxurious LNER, which ran from the 1920s to the 1940s. The ad lures riders with swirling trout, a tantalizing glimpse of a fly, and the promise to supply any patron with a copy of "Salmon and Trout Rivers Served by the LNER."*

*Swift water flows through a vibrant north woods landscape in "Trout Stream," an original watercolor painting by Minnesota artist Birney Quick (1912–1981). Quick helped found, in 1947, northern Minnesota's celebrated Grand Marais Art Colony. (Courtesy of the Minnesota Historical Society)*

of the joking earl and the serious widow, and, saving the [Horatio] Bottomley [fraud] case to read on the train going home, put the trout filled paper in your jacket pocket. There are great trout in the Canada du Rhone, and it is when the sun has dropped back of the mountains and you can fish down the stream with the evening breeze that they can be taken.

Fishing slowly down the edge of the stream, avoiding the willow trees near the water and the pines that run along the upper edge of what was once the old canal bank with your back cast, you drop the fly on to the water at every likely looking spot. If you are lucky, sooner or later there will be a swirl or a double swirl where the trout strikes and misses and strikes again, and then the old, deathless thrill of the plunge of the rod and the irregular plunging, circling, cutting up stream and shooting into the air fight the big trout puts up, no matter what country he may be in. It is a clear stream and there is no excuse for losing him when he is once hooked, so you tire him by working him against the current and then, when he shows a flash of white belly, slide him up against the bank and snake him up with a hand on the leader.

It is a good walk in to Aigle. There are horse chestnut trees along the road with their flowers that look like wax candles and the air is warm from the heat the earth absorbed from the sun. The road is white and dusty, and I thought of Napoleon's grand army, marching along it through the white dust on the way to the St. Bernard pass and Italy. Napoleon's batman may have gotten up at sun up before the camp and sneaked a trout or two out of the Rhone canal for the Little Corporal's breakfast. And before Napoleon, the Romans came along the valley and built this road and some Helvetian in the road gang probably used to sneak away from the camp in the evening to try for a big one in one of the pools under the willows. In the Roman days the trout perhaps weren't as shy.

So I went along the straight white road to Aigle through the evening and wondered about the grand army and the Romans and the Huns that traveled light and fast, and yet must have had time to try the stream along towards daylight, and very soon I was in Aigle, which is a very good place to be. I have never seen the town of Aigle, it straggles up the hillside, but there is a cafe across the station that has a galloping gold horse on top, a great wisteria vine as thick through as a young tree that branches out and shades the porch with hanging bunches of purple flowers that bees go in and out of all day long and that glisten after a rain; green tables with green chairs, and seventeen per cent dark beer. The beer comes foaming out in great glass mugs that hold a quart and cost forty centimes, and the barmaid smiles and asks about your luck.

Trains are always at least two hours apart in Aigle, and those waiting in the station buffet, this cafe with the golden horse and the wisteria hung porch is a station buffet, mind you, wish they would never come.

# *Big Secret Trout*

*By Robert Travers*

Attorney John Donaldson Voelker (1903–1991), writing under the penname Robert Travers, achieved international renown with the 1957 publication of his first novel, *Anatomy of a Murder*. The best-selling courtroom drama soon came to the big screen, and in 1960, Voelker retired from his position as a Michigan Supreme Court Justice, asserting, "Other people can write my opinions, but none can write my novels."

After retirement, Voelker devoted himself full-time to writing and fly fishing. A lifelong resident of Ishpeming, Michigan, Voelker was a passionate and proficient angler who stalked trout in the waters of the Upper Peninsula. His books include *Anatomy of a Fisherman* (1964), *Laughing Whitefish* (1965), and *Trout Magic* (1974).

Voelker once wrote that trout country is "invariably beautiful." Taken from his popular book *Trout Madness* (1960), this essay captures, with breathtaking precision, that beauty.

LEFT: *A mountain stream rushes past an angler selecting a fly. (Photograph © R. Valentine Atkinson)*

NO MISANTHROPIST, I must nevertheless confess that I like and frequently prefer to fish alone. Of course in a sense all dedicated fishermen must fish alone; the pursuit is essentially a solitary one; but sometimes I not only like to fish out of actual sight and sound of my fellow addicts, but alone too in the relaxing sense that I need not consider the convenience or foibles or state of hangover of my companions, nor subconsciously compete with them (smarting just a little over their success or gloating just a little over mine), nor, more selfishly, feel any guilty compulsion to smile falsely and yield them a favorite piece of water.

There is a certain remote stretch of river on the Middle Escanaba that I love to fish by myself; the place seems made of wonder and solitude. This enchanted stretch lies near an old deer-hunting camp of my father's. A cold feeder stream—"The Spawnshop," my father called it—runs through the ancient beaver meadows below the camp. After much gravelly winding and circling and gurgling over tiny beaver dams the creek gaily joins the big river a mile or so east of the camp. Not unnaturally, in warm weather this junction is a favorite convention spot for brook trout.

One may drive to the camp in an old car or a jeep but, after that, elementary democracy sets in; all fishermen alike must walk down to the big river—even the

*New Zealand's exotic waters beckon anglers to fly fish new waters, such as this hidden cove in Tongariro National Park. (Photograph © Erwin and Peggy Bauer)*

*A rushing stream courses through Big Thompson Canyon in this fishing scene, dating from the 1940s. (Courtesy of the Colorado Historical Society)*

arrogant new jeepocracy. Since my father died the old ridge trail has become overgrown and faint and wonderfully clogged with windfalls. I leave it that way. Between us the deer and I manage to keep it from disappearing altogether. Since this trail is by far the easiest and closest approach to my secret spot, needless to say few, secretive, and great of heart are the fishermen I ever take over it.

I like to park my old fish car by the camp perhaps an hour or so before sundown. Generally I enter the neglected old camp to look around and, over a devotional beer, sit and brood a little over the dear dead days of yesteryear, or perhaps morosely review the progressive decay of calendar art collected there during forty-odd years. And always I am amazed that the scampering field mice haven't carried the musty old place away, calendars and all.... Traveling light, I pack my waders and fishing gear—with perhaps a can or two of beer to stave off pellagra—and set off. I craftily avoid using the old trail at first (thus leaving no clue), charging instead into the thickest woods, using my rod case as a wand to part the nodding ferns for hidden windfalls. Then veering right and picking up the trail, I am at last on the way to the fabulous spot where my father and I used to derrick out so many trout when I was a boy.

Padding swiftly along the old trail—over windfalls, under others—I sometimes recapture the fantasies of my boyhood: once again, perhaps, I am a lithe young Indian brave—the seventh son of Chief Booze-in-the-Face, a modest lad who can wheel and shoot the eye out of a woodchuck at seventy paces—not bound riverward to capture a great copper-hued trout for a demure copper-hued maiden; or again, and more sensibly, I am returning from the river simply to capture the copper-hued maiden herself. But copper fish or Indian maid, there is fantasy in the air; the earth is young again; all remains unchanged: there is still the occasional porcupine waddling away, bristling and ridiculous; still the startling whir of a partridge; still the sudden blowing and thumping retreat of a surprised deer. I pause and listen stealthily. The distant blowing grows fainter and fainter, "*whew*" and again "*whew*," like wind grieving in the pines.

By and by the middle-aged fisherman, still gripped by his fantasies, reaches the outlet of the creek into the main river. Hm . . . no fish are rising. He stoops to stash a spare can of beer in the icy gravel, scattering the little troutlings. Then, red-faced and panting, he lurches up river through the brambles to the old deer crossing at the gravel ford. Another unseen deer blows and stamps—this time across the river. "*Whew*," the fisherman answers, mopping his forehead on his sleeve, easing off the packsack, squatting there batting mosquitoes and sipping his beer and watching the endless marvel of the unwinding river. The sun is low, most of the water is wrapped in shadow, a pregnant stillness prevails. Lo, the smaller fish are beginning to rise. Ah, there's a good one working! Still watching, he gropes in the bunch grass for his rod case. All fantasies are now forgotten.

Just above his shallow gravel ford there is a wide, slick, still-running and hopelessly unwadable expanse of deep water—a small lake within the river. I have never seen a spot quite like it. On my side of this pool there is a steep-sloping sandy bank surmounted by a jungle of tag alders. On the far opposite bank there is an abrupt, rocky, root-lined ledge lined with clumps of outcurving birches, rising so tall, their quivering small leaves glittering in the dying sun like a million tinkling tambourines. But another good fish rises, so to hell with the tambourines.... For in this mysterious pool dwell some of the biggest brown trout I know. This is my secret spot. Fiendishly evasive, these trout are not only hard to catch but, because of their habitat, equally hard to fish. The fisherman's trouble is double.

A boat or canoe invariably invokes mutiny and puts them down—at least any vessel captained by me. My most extravagant power casts from the ford below usually do the same or else fall short, though not always. The tall fly-catching tag alders on my side discourage any normal bank approach consistent with retaining one's sanity. (Hacking down the tag alders would not only be a chore, but would at once spoil the natural beauty of the place and erect a billboard proclaiming: BIG TROUT RESIDE HERE!) Across the way the steep rocky bank and the clusters of birches and tangled small stuff make it impossible properly to present a fly or to handle a decent trout if one could. The place is a fisherman's challenge and a fisherman's dream: lovely, enchanted, and endlessly tantalizing. I love it.

Across from me, closer to the other side and nicely out of range, there is a slow whirl-around of silky black water, endlessly revolving. Nearly everything floating into the pool—including most natural flies—takes at least one free ride around this lazy merry-go-round. For many insects it is frequently the last ride, for it is here that the fat tribal chieftains among the brown trout foregather at dusk to roll and cavort. Many a happy hour have I spent fruitlessly stalking these wise old trout. The elements willing, occasionally I even outwit one. Once last summer I outwitted two—all in the same ecstatic evening. Only now can I venture coherently to speak of it.

I had stashed my beer in the creek mouth as usual and had puffed my way through the tangle up to the deep pool. There they were feeding in the merry-go-round, *both* of them, working as only big trout can work—swiftly, silently, accurately—making genteel little pneumatic sounds, like a pair of rival dowagers sipping their cups of tea. I commanded myself to sit down and open my shaking can of beer. Above and below the pool as far as I could see the smaller brook trout were flashily feeding, but tonight the entire pool belonged to these two quietly ravenous pirates. "Slp, slp" continued the pair as I sat there ruefully wondering what a Hewitt or LaBranche or Bergman would do.

"They'd probably rig up and go fishin'," at length I sensibly told myself in an awed stage whisper. So I arose and with furious nonchalance rigged up, slowly, carefully, ignoring the trout as though time were a dime and there were no fish rising in the whole river, dressing the line just so, scrubbing out the fine twelve-foot leader with my bar of mechanic's soap. I even managed to whistle a tuneless obbligato to the steady "Slp, slp, slp. . . ."

And now the fly. I hadn't the faintest idea what fly to use as it was too shadowy and far away to even guess what they were taking. Suddenly I had the idea: I had just visited the parlor of Peterson, one of my favorite fly tiers, and had persuaded him to tie up a dozen exquisitely small palmer-tied creations on stiff gray hackle. I had got them for buoyancy to roll-cast on a certain difficult wooded pond. Why not try one here? Yet how on earth would I present it?

Most fishermen, including this one, cling to their pet stupidities as they would to a battered briar or an old jacket; and their dogged persistence in wrong methods and general wrongheadedness finally wins them a sort of grudging admiration, if not many trout. Ordinarily I would have put these fish down, using my usual approach, in about two casts of a squirrel's tail. Perhaps the sheer hopelessness of the situation gave me the wit to solve it. Next time I'll doubtless try to cast an anvil out to stun them. "The *only* controlled cast I can possibly make here," I muttered, hoarse with inspiration, "is a *roll* cast . . . yes—it's that or nothing,

*"Shimmering, Shining Florida Keys"—the iridescent beauty of the Keys is captured in this Millard Wells watercolor painting.*

*Glimmering green waters break for a feeding cutthroat trout. (Photograph © Jeff Henry/Roche Jaune Pictures, Inc.)*

Johnny me bye." If it is in such hours that greatness is born, then this was my finest hour.

Anyone who has ever tried successfully to roll-cast a dry fly under any circumstances, let alone cross-stream in a wide river with conflicting currents and before two big dining trout, knows that baby sitting for colicky triplets is much easier. For those who know not the roll cast, I shall simply say that it is a heaven-born cast made as though throwing an overhand half-hitch with a rope tied to a stick, no backcast being involved. But a roll cast would pull my fly under; a decent back cast was impossible; yet I had to present a floating fly. That was my little problem.

"Slp, slp, slp," went the trout, oblivious to the turmoil within me.

Standing on the dry bank in my moccasins I calmly stripped out line and kept rolling it upstream and inshore—so as not to disturb my quarry—until I figured my fly was out perhaps ten feet more than the distance between me and the steadily feeding trout. And that was plenty far. On each test cast the noble little gray hackle quickly appeared and rode beautifully. "God bless Peterson," I murmured. Then I began boldly to arc the cast out into the main river, gauging for distance, and then—suddenly—I drew in my breath and drew up my slack and rolled out the fatal business cast. This was it. The fly lit not fifteen feet upstream from the top fish—right in the down whirl of the merry-go-round. The little gray hackle bobbed up, circled a trifle uncertainly and then began slowly to float downstream like a little major. The fish gods had smiled.

*This real-photo postcard, postmarked 1950, depicts a bountiful harvest.*

Exultant, I mentally reordered three dozen precious little gray hackles. Twelve feet, ten feet, eight . . . holding my breath, I also offered up a tiny prayer to the roll cast. "Slp, slp . . ." The count-down continued—five feet, two feet, one foot, "slp"—and he was on.

Like many big browns, this one made one gorgeous dripping leap and bore down in a power dive, way deep, dogging this way and that like a bulldog shaking a terrier. Keeping light pressure, I coaxed rather than forced him out of the merry-go-round. Once out I let him conduct the little gray hackle on a subterranean tour and then—and then—I saw and heard his companion resume his greedy rise, "Slp, slp." *That* nearly unstrung me; as though one's fishing companion had yawned and casually opened and drunk a bottle of beer while one was sinking for the third time.

Like a harried dime-store manager with the place full of reaching juvenile delinquents, I kept trying to tend to business and avoid trouble and watch the sawing leader and the other feeding trout all at the same time. Then my trout began to sulk and bore, way deep, and the taut leader began to vibrate and whine like the plucked string of a harp. What if he snags a deadhead? I fretted. Just then a whirring half-dozen local ducks rushed upstream in oiled flight, banking away when they saw this strange tableau, a queer man standing there holding a straining hoop. Finally worried, I tried a little more pressure, gently pumping, and he came up in a sudden rush and rolled on his side at my feet like a length of cordwood. Then he saw his tormentor and was down and away again.

The nighthawks had descended to join the bats before I had him folded and dripping in the net, stone dead. "Holy old Mackinaw!" I said, numb-wristed and weak with conquest. A noisy whippoorwill announced dusk. I blew on my matted gray hackle and, without changing flies, on the next business cast I was on to his partner—the senior partner, it developed—which I played far into the night, the nighthawks and bats wheeling all about me. Two days later all three of us appeared in the local paper; on the front page, mind you. I was the one in the middle, the short one with the fatuous grin.

Next season I rather think I'll visit my secret place once or twice.

*This still life painting by artist and fishing guide Bob White captures the thrill of planning a faraway fishing trip.*

CHAPTER THREE

# Trout Fever

"WHAT MORE CAN A MAN DESIRE WHEN STANDING KNEE-DEEP IN A MOUNTAIN RIVER, ROD IN HAND, WITH TROUT ON THE RISE?"

*–Odell Shepard, "Thread of the River"*

# Mr. Theodore Castwell

George Edward MacKenzie Skues (1858–1949) earned his place in history by daring to pursue and publicize a groundbreaking idea—the concept of fly fishing with a nymph. Scorned by dry fly purists but called the "greatest liberator of the human mind in fly-fishing this century" by his admirers, Skues remained graceful yet persistent under scrutiny. He authored countless articles and several books on the subject, including *The Way of a Trout with a Fly* (1921), *Nymph Fishing for Chalk Stream Trout* (1939), and the posthumous *Itchen Memories* (1951).

Once upon a time, Skues wrote that dry fly fishing had become "a sort of religion," the irreverence of which "was regarded as a sort of sin against the Holy Ghost for which there was no remission." This story, his most famous, explores that sin with his trademark humor. It appears in his book *Side-Lines, Side-Lights and Reflections* (1932).

PREVIOUS PAGE, MAIN IMAGE: *Under a cloud-dotted sky, an angler braces himself against the current. (Photograph © Doug Stamm)*

PREVIOUS PAGE, INSET IMAGE: *Western photographer Charles Belden took this picture of his wife, Frances Phelps Belden, fly fishing circa 1925. The Beldens lived on the famous Pitchfork Ranch in Wyoming. (Courtesy of the American Heritage Center, University of Wyoming)*

LEFT: *Morning sun silhouettes an angler and his fly line against the majestic backdrop of Yellowstone National Park. (Photograph © Jeff Henry/Roche Jaune Pictures, Inc.)*

MR. THEODORE CASTWELL, having devoted a long, strenuous, and not unenjoyable life to hunting to their doom innumerable salmon, trout, and grayling in many quarters of the globe, and having gained much credit among his fellows for his many ingenious improvements in rods, flies, and tackle employed for that end, in the fullness of time died and was taken to his own place.

St. Peter looked up from a draft balance sheet at the entry of the attendant angel.

"A gentleman giving the name of Castwell. Says he is a fisherman, your Holiness, and has 'Fly-fishers' Club, London,' on his card."

"Hm-hm," says St. Peter. "Fetch me the ledger with his account." St. Peter perused it.

"Hm-hm," said St. Peter. "Show him in."

Mr. Castwell entered cheerfully and offered a cordial right hand to St. Peter. "As a brother of the angle—" he began.

"Hm-hm," said St. Peter.

"I am sure I shall not appeal to you in vain for special consideration in connection with the quarters to be assigned to me here."

"Hm-hm," said St. Peter. "I have been looking at your account from below."

"Nothing wrong with it, I hope," said Mr. Castwell.

"Hm-hm," said St. Peter. "I have seen worse. What sort of quarters would you like?"

"Well," said Mr. Castwell. "Do you think you could manage something in the way of a country cottage of the Test Valley type, with modern conveniences and, say, three-quarters of a mile of one of those pleasant chalk streams, clear as crystal, which proceed from out the throne, attached?"

"Why, yes," said St. Peter. "I think we can manage that for you. Then what about your gear? You must have left your fly rods and tackle down below. I see you prefer a light split cane of nine foot or so, with appropriate fittings. I will indent upon the Works Department for what you require, including a supply of flies. I think you will approve of our dressers' productions. Then you will want a keeper to attend you."

"Thanks awfully, your Holiness," said Mr. Castwell. "That will be first-rate. To tell you the truth, from the Revelations I read, I was inclined to fear that I might be just a teeny-weeny bit bored in heaven."

"In H-hm-hm," said St. Peter, checking himself.

It was not long before Mr. Castwell found himself alongside an enchantingly beautiful clear chalk stream, some fifteen yards wide, swarming with fine trout feeding greedily; and presently the attendant angel assigned to him had handed him the daintiest, most exquisite, light split cane rod conceivable—perfectly balanced with reel and line—with a beautifully damped tapered cast of incredible fineness and strength—and a box of flies of such marvelous trying as to be almost mistakable for the natural insects they were to simulate.

*Visitors to Oregon's Silver Falls State Park, which encompasses a temperate rainforest, fly fish in unparalleled surroundings. (Photograph © Dennis Frates)*

*Caught on an Alder wet fly, a brown trout erupts out of the river. (Photograph © Doug Stamm)*

Mr. Castwell scooped up a natural fly from the water, matched it perfectly from the fly box, and knelt down to cast to a riser putting up just under a tussock ten yards or so above him. The fly lit like gossamer, six inches above the last ring; and next moment the rod was making the curve of beauty. Presently, after an exciting battle, the keeper netted out a beauty of about two and a half pounds.

"Heavens!" cried Mr. Castwell. "This is something like."

"I am sure his Holiness will be pleased to hear it," said the keeper.

Mr. Castwell prepared to move upstream to the next riser when he became aware that another trout had taken up the position of that which he had just landed, and was rising. "Just look at that," he said, dropping instantaneously to his knee and drawing off some line. A moment later an accurate fly fell just above the neb of the fish, and instantly Mr. Castwell engaged in battle with another lusty fish. All went well, and presently the landing net received its two and a half pounds.

"A very pretty brace," said Mr. Castwell, preparing to move on to the next of the string of busy nebs which he had observed putting up round the bend.

As he approached the tussock, however, he became aware that the place from which he had just extracted so satisfactory a brace was already occupied by another busy feeder.

"Well, I'm damned!" cried Mr. Castwell. "Do you see that?"

"Yes, sir," said the keeper.

The chance of extracting three successive trout from the same spot was too attractive to be forgone, and once more Mr. Castwell knelt down and delivered a perfect cast to the spot. Instantly it was accepted and battle was joined. All held, and presently a third gleaming trout joined his brethren in the creel.

Mr. Castwell turned joyfully to approach the next riser round the bend. Judge, however, his surprise to find that once more the pit beneath the tussock was occupied by a rising trout, apparently of much the same size as the others.

"Heavens!" exclaimed Mr. Castwell. "Was there ever anything like it?"

"No, sir," said the keeper.

"Look here," said he to the keeper, "I think I really must give this chap a miss and pass on to the next."

"Sorry! It can't be done, sir. His Holiness would not like it."

"Well, if that's really so," said Mr. Castwell, and knelt reluctantly to his task.

Several hours later he was still casting to the same tussock.

"How long is this confounded rise going to last?" inquired Mr. Castwell. "I suppose it will stop soon?"

"No, sir," said the keeper.

"What, isn't there a slack hour in the afternoon?"

"No afternoon, sir."

"What? Then what about the evening rise?"

"No evening, sir," said the keeper.

"Well, I shall knock off now. I must have had about thirty brace from that corner."

"Beg pardon, sir, but his Holiness would not like that."

"What?" said Mr. Castwell. "Mayn't I even stop at night?"

"No night here, sir," said the keeper.

"Then do you mean that I have got to go on catching these damned two and a half pounders at this comer for ever and ever?"

The keeper nodded.

"Hell!" said Mr. Castwell.

"Yes," said his keeper.

# *Backyard Trout*

*By Burton Spiller*

Burton Lowell Spiller (1886-1973) was a prize-winning gladiolus farmer, a writer, a hunter, and a fisherman. Long celebrated as "the poet laureate of the ruffed grouse," Spiller penned the classic upland shooting book, *Grouse Feathers* (1935), followed on the heels by *Thoroughbred* (1936), *Firelight* (1937), and *More Grouse Feathers* (1938).

Spiller also contributed over one hundred essays and stories to sporting magazines such as *Field & Stream*. In 1962, the best of these were collected into *Drummer in the Woods* (1962). Recently, Derrydale Press resurrected another set of his articles into *Grouse Feathers, Again* (2000).

In the last months of his life, Spiller compiled his final book, *Fishin' Around* (1974), his only volume devoted to the sport of angling. As with his grouse shooting stories, this essay is imbued with Spiller's signature warmth and humor.

LEFT: *"The rest of the world's trout may be taken in summer, to the sound of birds and the pleasant hum of insects, but the steelhead—the big, sea-going rainbow of the Northwest coasts—is winter's child."—Paul O'Neil, "Excalibur: The Steelhead," 1957 (Photograph © Dennis Frates)*

"TOMORROW," I SAID, as I kicked the cat down the cellar stairs and reached for the clock key, "marks the first day of spring, Can you imagine it?"

My wife regarded me with some anxiety. "Have you gone completely cuckoo?" she asked. "Spring began six weeks ago."

"Not by my calendar," I assured her. "Spring begins the first day of open season on trout. That's tomorrow."

"Good heavens!" she exclaimed. "Just when I was beginning to feel the least bit acquainted with you. Now I suppose I won't see any more of you until July."

"August," I corrected her. "I'll look you up sometime after August 15."

"Where are you going—and when do you start?"

I drew off my slippers and began undoing my tie. "As a matter of fact," I told her, "I can't get away for at least a week, and I'll have to work like the devil to make it in that time."

*An angler prepares to try the petite Hexagenia fly on California's Fall River. (Photograph © R. Valentine Atkinson)*

Just then the doorbell rang. I slipped into my bathrobe and answered it. It was my neighbor, Jonesie, and he seemed excited.

"What's the matter?" I asked, as I drew him into the hall. "Somebody sick? The baby—"

"No," he said. "Everybody's all right, but I just got a telegram. They've been rising all day on the big river. Let's go up there."

"I can't," I said. "Not for a week anyway. I'm too busy."

"Just for a day," he pleaded. "You can spare one day."

"It's too cold," I countered. "And it's too far up there. We would miss the morning fishing."

"It will be warmer tomorrow; the radio said so. 'Fair and warmer.' We could start now and be on the river by daylight."

"What? Start now? At eleven? Ride all night, fish all day and then ride home again? No, thank you. I'm through doing stunts like that."

Jonesie sighed regretfully. "I suppose you are right," he said. "When a fellow gets to be your age he has to be careful."

"My age? What do you mean, my age? I'm a year younger than you."

"In years, perhaps. I was thinking of your physical condition."

"There's nothing wrong with my physical condition," I yelled at him. "It is too early to fish the big river. We could take more trout, and better trout, right here around town than we could up there at this time of year."

"Always fishing in your own doorway," he accused me. "If you want to take trout you have to go where they are."

"Yes," I agreed. "And you also have to go when they are

rising. It's too early. There's still a lot of snow up there. I'm, too busy. I'm not going."

The rascal grinned. "I was thinking about the big one you lost up there last spring. In the pool below the falls. You remember? I thought perhaps you might like to tie into him again before someone else did. Boy, was that a battle! My heart turned completely over when he went down through the rips. Well, I'm sorry you can't make it, but I think I'll go just the same. I'd sure like to fight it out with that baby. I'd show him who was the boss."

*The trout-rich waters of Fancy Creek wind through rural Wisconsin. (Photograph © Doug Stamm)*

"Look," I said. "Maybe you could handle him better than I did, and maybe you couldn't, but if you get the chance to try it you'll have to lay a better fly than I can. Go home and get your car and tackle. In twenty minutes I'll be ready to go up there and give you a fishing lesson."

The eastern sky was only faintly pink when we parked the car in a gravel pit near the lower falls. The headlights played on some empty tar barrels and they looked suspiciously white. I stepped out of the car to investigate, and the air cut like a knife. As I had suspected, there was a quarter inch of frost on the barrels. I got back into the car where I could shiver more comfortably while I razzed Jonesie.

"Yah!" I jeered. "Fair and warmer, eh? I'll bet you forgot to bring an ice chisel."

"It'll warm up," he promised. "As soon as the sun gets up it will be all right. Let's take a nap."

Sleep, I knew, was impossible, but I thought it would be a good plan to rest my eyes for a few minutes—and when I opened them again, the sun was shining, the car windows were white with rime, and my legs were numb and lifeless.

"Come on," I yelled to Jonesie, and shook him savagely. "Let's get out of here before we freeze to death."

Hastily we assembled our rods and drew on our waders, our teeth chattering and our fingers all thumbs as we fumbled with our fly books. As we climbed down the embankment to the pool the grass crunched crisply underfoot. We paused at last on the twenty-foot ledge and peered down into the turbulent water. Then Jonesie pointed with a trembling forefinger and I looked in the direction it indicated.

It was a bit downstream from where we stood, an elongated, seemingly quiet place in the rushing water, and beneath it the gravel bottom of the pool would have

*This vintage catalog cover is from L. L. Bean, the ultimate in fly fishing clothiers.*

been plainly visible had it not been for the fact that at least fifty—I swear it!—trout obscured it from our startled gaze. I could feel my pulse accelerate, and was aware of a sudden and pleasing warmth. The trout were lying in about ten feet of water, but despite the dwarfing effect they looked big.

"Jonesie," I said, "this is the day when we justify our existence. I'm going to put a curve in this rod that a chiropractor couldn't straighten with a ten-pound hammer."

An hour later I began to wonder if I had not, perhaps, spoken too hastily. Two hours later I had come to the conclusion that it would have been better if I had refrained from speaking at all. An hour after that I began to feel that the proper time for saying something pertinent to the occasion was rapidly approaching. I began arranging words and phrases, but before I had them grouped to my liking Jonesie beat me to it. He must have been dwelling on it for hours, for he rose to sublime heights. The trout endured it for a few moments, shrinking together at each withering blast, then dashed upstream as a single unit.

"There, dash blank 'em!" he said. "They've gone and I'm glad of it. I've offered them every fly in the book and not a dad-burned one of them would so much as look at it."

It occurred to me to say, "I told you so," but I had the impression that to do so would be invoking an unnecessary risk. Presently I saw him glumly untying his leader. Silently I did likewise, reeled in the line, and unjointed the rod. Then, side by side, as mournfully silent as though we were a part of a funeral cortege, we walked back to the car.

Within a mile of my home the road runs for a few rods close beside a brook which once was excellent trout water. Where it turns to pursue its wandering way through heavy woods, an excellent pool has formed. The upper end is shallow enough to wade, but the lower half is satisfyingly deep, while an old pine on the bank affords it perfect shade. Many a time I have slipped out there for an hour just after sunset and taken a trout or two from under the abrupt bank. Native brook trout, they were, plump and firm, and red-fleshed as only native trout can be.

As we wheeled past it my eye swept the surface of the pool. It was only a momentary glance, but in the shadow cast by the old pine I saw a slight disturbance on the water, and around it a ring suddenly formed and slowly spread. I opened my mouth to speak, then closed it as an idea began taking shape in my mind.

When he left me in my driveway Jonesie said, "Well, this has just been another one of those days, but we've at least inhaled a lot of fresh air. There's one thing certain, though. If you get 'em you have to go after 'em. You can't catch 'em by fishing in your own backyard."

I waited until he was out of sight, then unlocked the garage, stowed my equipment in the car, and drove out to the pool. The sun had set, and under the pine the water looked dark and mysterious. Even while I was tying on a small streamer a trout broke in the shadows.

Wading out in the shallow end of the pool, I worked out line and flipped the fly toward the deeper water. My cast was purposely short, for I wanted to fish the nearer part first, in hope that at least one trout would be cruising the shallows.

I had retrieved scarcely a yard of line when I saw that welcome, silvery flash, and as I flipped the rod tip upward I felt the hook slide home. Stripping in a few yards of line, I forced him to fight in the shallows, playing him as gently as possible in order to keep the disturbance down to a minimum.

*Folks clamor to see the clear spring-fed waters coursing through the heart of historic Bellefonte, Pennsylvania. The handwritten message on this real-photo postcard, postmarked July 1936, reads: "You should see the trout in this place. If the cops wouldn't get me I would fish right here."*

Two minutes later I slid the net under him and was pleasantly surprised to find that he was larger than I had thought. The rule showed him to be eleven inches, and the blood-red spots along his sides proclaimed him to be a native, a survivor of that rapidly diminishing clan of river trout that formerly ran the brook from the time of the first spring freshets until the spawning season had ended in the fall.

Slipping him into the creel, I once more laid the fly along the edge of the deeper water. The cast was unrewarded, but on the next one I had a smashing rise. Once more we fought it out in the shallow water, and even while we were doing so I saw a fish break in the center of the pool, and heard a hearty splash from the deep shadows under the pine.

*They're growing bigger and better*, I thought, as I laid the rule on this one and found it lacked but a hair of being a full foot in length.

Again a fish rose, well out toward the center of the pool, but I drew him in with another purposely short cast. A smaller fish than the others, or so I judge, and the rule proved my guess to be correct. Only ten inches, but as I slid him into the basket I could feel it assume a bit of weight.

Carefully I covered all the nearer water, then lengthened line and laid the fly well out in the center of the pool.

*Wham!* When I set the hook in this one I knew I was fast to a fish. I invited him to come up in the shallows where we could fight it out man to man, but he was opposed to the idea. It was evident that he regarded that hole under the bank as Home Sweet Home, and he had a nostalgic longing to return to it, but I vetoed that proposition.

Back and forth across the pool he went; now fighting deeply in an effort to regain his coveted sanctuary, now threshing the water to foam as he splashed on the surface. Tiring at last, he permitted me to lead him into the knee-deep water, and a minute later he came to net. My twelve-inch rule was far too short to determine his length, but I noticed that when I laid him in my fifteen-inch basket his nose and tail touched the willow. With the addition of this one to the creel, the strap began to sag comfortably upon my shoulder.

As I once more whipped the fly across the pool I noticed that the shadows were deepening perceptibly. Under the high bank it was no longer possible to see the fly; consequently I missed a good rise, but hooked him on the next cast. This time he fought it out in the deep water. If the commotion the big fellow made had not disturbed them, it seemed unlikely that this one would seriously alarm any that might remain in the pool.

The figures on the rule were not deeply etched, but I thought the length of this one to be ten inches. When he was stowed away I hesitated and stole a glance at the sky. In the west a thin crescent of moon hung precariously, while in the east I caught the faint twinkle of the first star. It was time to quit, but the urge to make one more cast was too strong to resist. I worked out line and shot it toward the towering bank.

Even through the thickening dark I could see the creamy foam when his broad tail lashed the water, and I struck in anticipation of the forthcoming tug. It did not materialize, and reluctantly I began stripping in line.

Then he hit it. *Zowie!* What a smash. I wonder why it is that darkness causes one's imagination to run riot. Reason told me that this fish was no larger than the big one in the basket, but I found it hard to believe. Its dashes seemed stronger, and the pull on my wrist greater. Even the possibility that I might lose him became magnified in my mind until it assumed the proportion of a major calamity.

After minutes that seemed interminable, I worked him into the shallow and at last I had him in the net. The creel was a trifle narrower at the top and it was necessary to bend the fish into a bow in order to close the cover.

Back home once more, I went down to the basement and laid the beauties out on the cold cement in a straight line, the tail of one just touching the nose of another. Then I unfolded a six-foot rule and placed it beside them. The six fish measured 71 inches, an average of approximately 11¾ inches each.

I gloried over them for a few minutes, then replaced them in the creel, slung it over my shoulder, and went down to Jonesie's house. Through the window I could see that he was about to retire. Even as I looked he snapped a half-consumed cigarette into the fireplace, yawned, and got stiffly to his feet.

As I hooked the creel strap over the doorknob, I thought, *Jonesie is a mighty good fisherman and a mighty good friend. If he were not, I'd never risk doing what I'm going to do now.*

With that, I gave the bell a vicious jab, heard it shatter the silence within, saw Jonesie straighten and turn toward the door, and then I fled down the steps and into the concealing darkness of the night.

*Dense overgrowth and a flowing stream lend quietude to this Richard Vander Meer painting. Using oils, watercolor, and pastel, Vander Meer specializes in fishing-themed works.*

# Potter's Fancy

By Corey Ford

During the Roaring Twenties, a young satirist named Corey Ford (1902–1969) landed his literary burlesques in the pages of such esteemed publications as the *New Yorker*, *Vanity Fair*, and *Life*. Parodying everyone from Robert Frost to William Faulkner, Ford became famous for his lampooning wit.

After the 1929 stock market crash, a brief career as a Hollywood screenwriter, and a stint in the Air Force, Ford settled in rural New Hampshire. Here, he found the characters to inspire his hilarious *Field & Stream* column, "Minutes of the Lower Forty."

Ford's stories are collected in several books, including *You Can Always Tell a Fisherman: The Minutes of the Lower Forty Shooting, Angling and Inside Straight Club* (1958) and *Uncle Perk's Jug: The Misadventures of the Lower Forty Shooting, Angling, and Inside Straight Club* (1964). In all, the prolific Ford authored thirty books and roughly 500 magazine articles.

This irreverent "Lower Forty" installment features Uncle Perk, his ubiquitous jug of Old Stump Blower, and an inebriated fly fisherman named Perley Potter.

LEFT: *Fishermen consult their fly boxes before entering Wyoming's Flat Creek. (Photograph © R. Valentine Atkinson)*

*The whiskey is poured and the waders hung out to dry in this vintage Paul Jones advertisement.*

THEIR TROUT RODS rested horizontally on nails driven in the side of Cousin Sid's camp, their wet waders hung from pegs, and the members of the Lower Forty lounged on the granite doorstep, basking in the warm June sun. The pleasant aroma of luncheon wafted from the kitchen, where Cousin Sid was frying the results of their early morning's catch. Uncle Perk reached for his jug of Old Stump Blower, and then hid it hurriedly behind a clump of ferns as a canvas-clad figure stumbled along the path toward them, weaving slightly. "Mornin', Perley," Uncle Perk greeted him.

"Mornin'," Perley Potter replied, lowering the battered fishing rod he carried over his shoulder and leaning against a tree for support.

"Think that big trout of yours will be rising this soon in the day?" Doc Hall asked.

"Figgered I'd git to the pool a mite early," Perley explained in a husky voice, "in case he gits hongry ahead o' time." He rubbed the back of a hand across his stubbled chin. "Don't s'pose you fellers got a little somethin' to wet my whistle," he pleaded. "I seem to've picked up one o' these hangovers that's been runnin' around lately."

"Sorry, Perley," Uncle Perk said firmly, "we ain't got a drop."

"Wal, in that case," Perley sighed, "I guess I'll be movin' along. Can't never tell when ole Beelzebub might show up." He stooped to grasp his rod, and the neck of a pint flask protruded from his hip pocket. The Lower Forty exchanged silent glances as he staggered up the path, tacking from side to side and caroming off an occasional oak.

"Sure hate to see a nice feller like Perley let himself go that way," Uncle Perk grumbled. "Used to be a real hard-workin' cuss till he took to drink."

"What started him off?" Colonel Cobb inquired.

"If you ast me, it's that tarnation trout," Uncle Perk replied. "Ever since he spotted Beelzebub a coupla years ago, he's been goin' from bad to worst. All he thinks about is catchin' that fish. He broods about it so much that he takes a drink before he starts fishin', an' then if he misses a strike he has to take another drink to console himself, an' by that time he's so orry-eyed he can't see to cast a fly, which depresses him till he has to have another drink, an' when he wakes up the fishin' is all over, so then he gets real drunk to drownd his sorrows."

"Suppose it would cure him if he caught it?" Doc Hall mused.

"He'll never catch a smart ole devil like Beelzebub unless he sobers up," Uncle Perk grunted, "an' he'll never sober up unless he catches it." He recovered the jug from its hiding place among the ferns and took a swallow. "It's the curse o' the demon rum."

"Stingeth like the adder," Judge Parker agreed, reaching for the jug, "and biteth like the serpent."

*An angler tests his long, flexible fly rod in California's Pit River. (Photograph © R. Valentine Atkinson)*

Doc Hall borrowed the jug in turn. "Look not upon the wine when it is red," he nodded solemnly, and handed it to Mister MacNab.

"Pairsonally I never touch a drop myself," Mister MacNab said, "unless it's fr-r-ree." He lowered the jug after a long moment. "'Tis a fortunate thing we dinna suffer the same cur-r-rse as poor Pairley."

The afternoon hatch of flies was just starting as the Lower Forty, rods in hand, hurried up the path along the stream. They came to Perley Potter's favorite pool, and Doc Hall paused and pointed. Perley was stretched at the base of a dead stump, his fishing rod on the grass beside him, the pint bottle tilted to his lips. His face was downcast. "What happened, Perley?" Doc asked.

"Missed him again," Perley mourned. "He was risin' over by that far bank, an' I tried to make a cast an' hooked my fly on a hemlock an' fell into the pool an' scairt him away." His trembling fingers worked in vain to tie on another fly. "Here, mebbe you can make this thing quit jigglin' up and down," he said to Doc.

Doc Hall threaded Perley's leader through the eye of the hook and knotted it. "What's this fly called?" he asked curiously, inspecting the bedraggled woolen body dressed with chicken feathers.

"It's s'posed to be Potter's Fancy," Perley sighed, "but nowadays my hand shakes so I can't tie 'em like I used to." He consoled himself with another swig from his flask, and closed his eyes. "You fellers go ahead," he murmured, "I'll wait here fer ole Beelzebub."

Perley was still reclining at the base of the stump, his fishing rod beside him, when Doc and the others made their way back down the path at dusk. His bottle was empty, his mouth hung open, and he emitted a steady gurgling snore. Doc gazed at him in sympathy, and his eye wandered toward the stream. Suddenly he froze, staring at a small bump which appeared momentarily in the flat run over by the far bank. "Perley!" he shouted, "get your rod, quick!"

Uncle Perk peered at the slumbering figure. "He wouldn' wake up if it was half-past doomsday."

Another newly-hatched fly dropped down from the overhanging grass bank and was caught in the dark run. Again the bump showed for an instant in the smooth water, leaving barely a ripple as the insect disappeared. Doc scooped up a spent fly from the eddy at his feet and studied it a moment. "Olive dun," he nodded. He opened his fly box and riffled the contents. "This one ought to do it," he decided, "about No. 16." He tied the artificial dun on his leader, glanced once more at the inert form beside the stump, and crept cautiously toward the stream.

His first cast fell short, and he let his fly drift well below the feeding trout before he retrieved it, lifting it slightly off the water with an expert flick of his rod tip. Again he shot the line forward, stripping another foot or so from his reel. The fly lit on a tuft of grass, toppled into the run, and rode downstream. Something rolled under it, the fly was sucked out of sight, and Doc waited a fraction of a second and then tightened. A huge V raced across the pool, his reel screamed, and there was a heavy swirl and the glimpse of a green slab-side turning. Perley stirred slightly, a dreamy smile crossed his face, and he settled back in deep repose.

Doc Hall leapt in to the stream, his arched rod held high, and followed the speeding trout around a bend of the stream. A half hour passed before he returned up the path, carrying the monster squaretail curled in his landing net. "It's the grandaddy of them all," he gloated. "Ought to go four or five pounds."

"We'll take it back to the store an' weigh it," Uncle Perk suggested.

Doc shook his head. "This is Perley's trout," he said quietly. He took Beelzebub from the net, reached for Perley's leader, and hooked Potter's Fancy securely in the trout's jaw. He laid the fish on the grass beside the sleeping form, paused in thought for a moment, and then scooped some water in his hat and poured it over Perley's extended waders. Perley never stirred as the Lower Forty tiptoed down the trail toward Cousin Sid's camp.

Late that night they heard someone stumbling along the path, and the pounding of a fist on the front door. Perley Potter lurched into the room, his eyes bloodshot, holding the trout by its gills. "B'gorry, I got 'im," he said thickly. "Cotched him on Potter's Fancy."

"Put up a good fight?" Doc asked, with a wink at the others.

*The Wind River Mountains make a stately backdrop for a fly fishing trip in Wyoming. (Photograph © Erwin and Peggy Bauer)*

"Hmmm? Yeah. Yeah, I guess so." Perley's face had a blank look, as though he had stopped to worship at a wayside shrine and been hit on the head by a falling plaster angel. "My waders was wet clear up to the waist. Yeah, it must of been the fight of a lifetime."

"Wal, congratulations, Perley," Uncle Perk beamed, removing the cork from the jug of Old Stump Blower. "How about a little somethin' to celebrate?"

Perley leapt back as though he had stepped on a copperhead. "Not for me. I'll never tetch another drop as long as I live."

Uncle Perk blinked. "Wotinell's come over you?"

"I learnt my lesson," Perley said in a quavering voice. "All these years I been dreamin' about the time I'd cotch that trout, and now I done it, an' I don't remember anything about it." Tears welled in his eyes. "Biggest thrill I'll ever have, an' I missed the whole fun." His voice broke. "Now I'll never know what it was like."

He held the trout aloft, and gazed dolefully into its glazed eyes.

"I'm gonna have him mounted an' hang him on the wall," he sobbed, "an' any time I'm tempted to take a drink I'll look up at Beelzebub an' remind myself. Never again."

The door closed, and they heard his uncertain steps recede down the path. Uncle Perk picked up the jug of Old Stump blower, strode resolutely into the kitchen, and poured the remaining contents down the sink. Mister MacNab emitted a strangled sound.

"What ever-r-r are ye doing, mon?" he gasped.

"In memory of Beelzebub," Uncle Perk replied. There was a moment of respectful silence. "Besides," he added, "they's another full jug right out in the car."

# *I, Fisherman*

*By George Tichenor*

George Tichenor (1906-1959) was committed to the labor movement, serving as editor for a variety of newsletters, including the Eastern Cooperative League's *Cooperator*; the International Brotherhood of Electrical Workers' *Spotlight*; and the Hat, Cap, and Millinery Workers' *Hat Worker*. As part of the largely Jewish hat-makers' union, Tichenor wrote articles on many social and economic issues, including anti-Semitism, industry competition, and inflation.

Tichenor also penned creative prose, including two novels, *Glibson* (1933) and *Manhattan Prodigal* (1934). His essays and fiction appeared in magazines such as *Hound and Horn* and *Outdoor Life*.

An enthusiastic angler, Tichenor wrote this essay for the May 1953 issue of *Outdoor Life*. A newcomer to the grand world of fishing with a fly, he self deprecates with cheerful aplomb and presents a hilarious vision of learning to cast a fly line on the revered Willowemoc.

LEFT: *Equipped for a day's fishing, a lone angler prowls an overgrown bank in this original work by painter Richard Vander Meer.*

THERE'S ONE THING I enjoy doing, and it's showing up the experts. And the second is like unto it—talking about it afterward. I belong to the school of "They Laughed When I Rose to Speak," or "They Little Knew When I Sat Down to the Piano." That's me. The natural genius with hook and line, for instance: Or at least I thought so . . . until I took up fishing.

It all started the day I dropped into OUTDOOR LIFE headquarters and got to talking with P. Allen Parsons, associate editor, about a bug I saw lying on his desk. He said it was a Fly, not to be swatted, and the more he talked about it the more intensity crept into his voice; I realized I was in the presence of a man in need of the fishermen's equivalent of Alcoholics Anonymous.

In three minutes he had me worked up too, and if he hadn't hidden that thing away one of us would have snapped at it. It occurred to me that artificial flies could be cheap substitute for live bait, and that fishing could be an inexpensive harmless sport. Yeah, that's what I thought, and I saw myself casually sending some friend a couple of king-size trophies, resting on a bed of glittering ice that would look just right in Tiffany's window. And I could hear the friend's wife saying, when they had recovered from their surprise, "Isn't that just like George? He does everything with such Natural Grace."

With the bashfulness of a sea lion at feeding time, I put myself in the way of an invitation to learn the ropes of fly fishing. P. A. paled but had the courage of a born sportsman. He said he'd take me along.

When I mentioned our date to Al Smoke, the accountant in our office, he was struck with admiration; you could have turned him over with a stick. For besides being fond of fishing, Al follows what P. A. says in print. I wanted Al to see how a beginner could make monkeys out of experts, so I cleared through channels and he became a third member of our party.

On a day late in May I arose at 5:30 to get the car, pick up Smoke, and hie to Livingston Manor, which is about 110 miles from New York City, and a fishing spot in the Catskills. Al, with his boodle, was lurking in the shadow of his apartment as I drove up. He hopped in, I gunned the accelerator, and we roared off, not too soon to hear one of his kids at the window: "There they go, mom; the jerk from the office is driving the get-away car."

In due time we arrived at Clarence Wright's place, which is up a narrow winding road, almost hidden (so as not to attract tourists), and country-folksy as a Currier and Ives print. It's one of those gingerbread American Gothic farmhouses, with a comforting clatter from the kitchen, an old dog lolling under a tree, and two black kittens popping in and out of boots against the wall.

Clarence, in short boots and a battered hat cocked on the side of his head, is as characteristically Yankee as a Winesap apple. He gave us a crisp welcome and a vigorous handshake. He and P. A. (who had just arrived) plunged into fish talk, and all of us wasted not a minute but pushed into boots and waders, stomping and strapping them on, anxious to get going before the stream dried up. My waders—

borrowed from Al, who'd promised to provide other gear as well—looked like the rear end of a gray horse that had been skinned with a dull knife.

For the benefit of those who came in late, I'll pause to explain what we were after. Maybe, like myself, you've thought that fishing is just a matter of hook, line, and sinker. Or the way they did it in the mountains of Georgia where I grew up. They filled a demijohn with lye, inserted a cork loosely, and tossed it in a stream. The cork came out, soon there was a boom, and the fish came up.

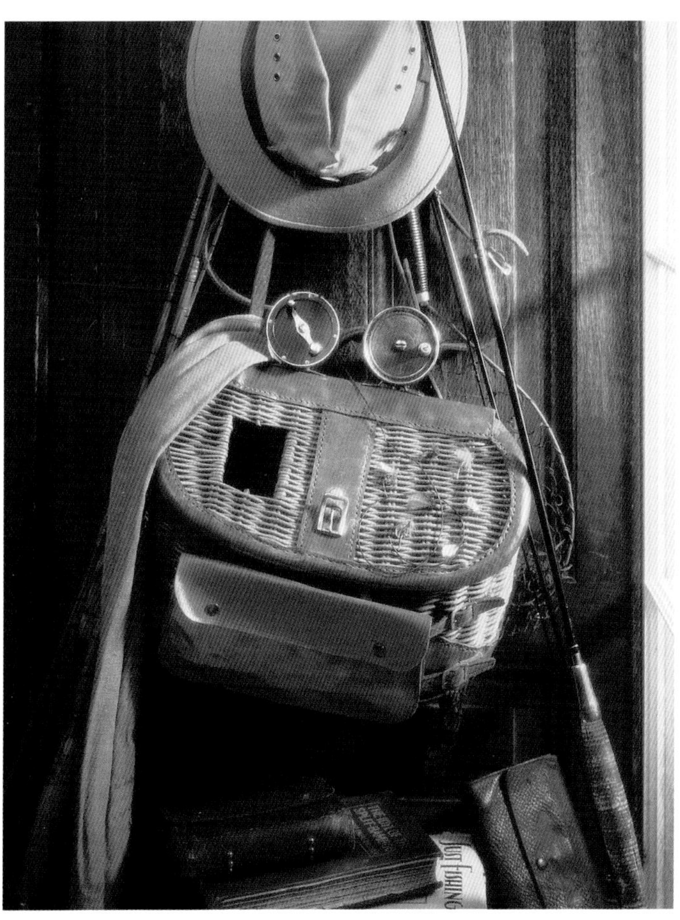

*An angler hangs his hat and creel until the next trip to the river. (Photograph © Howard Lambert)*

Well, it's not so simple as that. In the circles where I'm now moving even the Marquis of Queensberry would have difficulty in observing all the rules.

I have learned that fishermen are graded according to the size of fish they catch. The lowest and most vulgar type (according to stream fishermen) are those who go in for tuna and other deep-sea stuff. As a trout man explained to me not long ago: "There's nothing to it. They bait a hook with meat"—here a special grimace of distaste—"and toss it over; the tuna grabs it and sounds. Then it's just like hauling coal up an elevator shaft."

Going higher in the piscatorial kingdom, there are those who fish for pickerel, pike, bass . . . and, at the top of the ladder . . . trout! But wait, I'm not finished. There are also grades of trout fishermen. There is the low criminal element that uses worms ("The sort who'd put a scorpion in a baby's crib," the man said). And there are spinners, wet-fly . . . and ultimately dry-fly men. P. A., of course, was strictly High Church.

All too soon, I was rigged out in the waders Al had lent me. They were Navy surplus, minus a diving helmet. The lead plates had been removed from the soles, and Al told me comfortingly this gave the feet a tendency to float. In addition to suspenders, there was a drawstring arrangement near my middle that worked like the mouth of a laundry bag. Below the waist I was well protected, but if a trout had leapt at me from above, I would have been done for.

I felt like the rear end of a stage horse, but Al kept piling stuff on me in a mournful manner. You see, he's an accountant and keeps track of everything. He

# TROUT TRUTHS

A cutthroat trout hovers enticingly in Yellowstone River near Fishing Bridge, once a hotspot of fly fishing, now delegated to observation of the finny critters. (Photograph © Jeff Henry/Roche Jaune Pictures, Inc.)

WHAT IS THE best season of the year to go a-fishing?

I think the best time is when you feel like it and can leave home and business. The desire for fishing is like some diseases, in attacking a man with great severity without notice. It can be no more resisted than falling in love can be resisted, and, like love, the best treatment is its gratification.

What is the best time o'day for fishing?

Any time after breakfast. Never go before, for trout are not early risers. I have known men to get out of bed at daylight, making much noise, to the disgust of those who wished to sleep, and rush off with an empty stomach save perhaps for a drink of whiskey, and return several hours later to a cold breakfast, having captured nothing but a headache. Trout will bite just when they feel like it, and the best way to ascertain their biting time is to give them a frequent opportunity.

How about the wind and the weather?

Trout will bite when the wind blows and when it does not. A cloudy day is best except when they rise better on a bright, sunny one. They also often bite well when it rains.

What fly is best?

The fly the trout seem to fancy most on the day you are out. I never go without at least fifty varieties. You may as well ask a woman what style of bonnet she prefers. The taste of trout and women is governed by a similar law, and they change it quite as often. I once made a fly that was so ugly that it frightened my cat out of the room, and yet it proved a great killer. The surest way is to have every known specimen, and to try them all.

What kind of hook is best?

The one with a sharp point, and when you miss a trout charge your clumsiness to the hook and say you prefer some other make.

As conditions are innumerable, it is difficult to make rules to-day which will not fail to-morrow. My advice is—go often and visit many localities. Kill no more fish than you require for your own eating, and do that in the most scientific manner. A trout is a gentleman, and should be treated as such and lured with only delicate and humane weapons.

*—Charles Barker Bradford, The Brook Trout and the Determined Angler, 1900*

*You can lead a man to water, but you can't make him land a trout.*

*"I rummaged through my fly case with dancing hands. A sixteen-inch brook trout seized the fly before it touched the water." –E. Annie Proulx, "Somewhere With Sven," 1993 (Photograph © Doug Stamm)*

finally announced, "You have about $75 worth of equipment on you," and I knew he'd be sorry to see me step into quicksand, disappearing inch by inch, dollar by dollar.

We moved off, Al very natty in high brown boots, P. A. and I slogging along in waders.

The Willowemoc, which we were going to fish, is a famous trout stream. It was hereabouts that Theodore Gordon introduced the dry fly to this country with a batch of imitation insects he got from England in 1890. Before then trout were caught the way you'd expect, with a w---m on a hook, or wet flies, and neither fish nor fishermen got neurotic about it. But brown trout, which also came over from England–in 1883, probably on a ship called the Mayfly–proved to be suckers for insects. Between Gordon's flies and the brown trout, a new era of the Light Touch was born, with a whole new generation of fishermen to match. Watch P. A. in action, as I did, and you begin to get the idea.

P. A. approaches the stream with a thrust-forward gait, pipe jutting from his jaw. Let others think of the spring day and lissom lads and lassies; he knows there's man's work to be done.

In a quiet voice, so as not to alarm the pink-cheeked recruits who have never witnessed battle, he now discussed the Insect Situation with Al. They looked at the rushing water, which looked like plain water to me, and agreed that the shadfly hatch was past. May flies were due, but the water was just about right for a hatch of blue flies. But the temperature was only 38° F., and P. A. shook his head ominously. "Sixty to 65 would be just right." I gathered it would be difficult to connect with a fish, even on a pre-heated hook. But the sun was fine, and I was almost chuckling about what would happen to those poor unsuspecting trout when my fine Italian hand presented an offering.

P. A. took out his fly box and he and Al bent over it eagerly. To be frank–and not for publication–I told myself I'd as soon reach my hand into a busted horsehair sofa and pull out a bunch of stuffing. But I was mildly interested when P. A. selected a fly with long hackles made of deer hair, touched it up with water repellent from a bitty bottle, and then attached it to a nylon leader about as fine as the hair on your head. The line wasn't much thicker, and the split-bamboo rod was like a long switch.

P. A. moved out into the swirling water and began to shake out the line, not quite over his head, not quite sideways. (This part I can't explain. I watched it. It seemed as rhythmic and effortless as a bit of ballet dancing.) Slowly, then accelerando. The yellow line lengthened with each swish until it was about 40 feet long. Then P.A. "presented" the fly as though it were a live insect, alighting in a little pool and caught up by a swirl of water. The fly came floating down. Leader and line were invisible, without too much slack, pulled in by the quick fingers of a veteran as the lure drifted toward him. Then he raised it up and tried again, to the same spot . . . and again. Never a slop. Surely any trout down among the rocks, however doubtful that a hatch was on, would be convinced upon seeing four or five flies in succession alight, with nary a shadow of leader or line.

ABOVE: *Aristocratic fly fishers seem to dance on the shore in this James Pollard painting dating from the 1830s. A prominent English sporting artist, Pollard dedicates the image "to the Members of the Waltonian Society, by a Brother Angler."*

LEFT: *Victorian fly fishers cast competitive glares in this vintage postcard illustrated by F. Earl Christy, whose artwork appeared on countless postcards, advertisements, and magazine covers in the early 1900s.*

*A pair of anglers survey a stretch of the Snake River, purple mountains rising in the distance. (Photograph © R. Valentine Atkinson)*

O.K., I said, I'll do the same. We were strung out about a quarter of a mile by now, for no fisherman likes anyone nudging his elbow. At a point below P. A., me and the waders slithered into the water, with a splash no larger than the launching of the U.S.S. Missouri. The cold came through instantly, swift water gripped my legs, the rocky bottom seemed to be greased—and my invaluable head began wobbling above my thrashing arms and shoulders. I'd have called the whole thing off, if someone had sent a breeches buoy my way, as they do in the newsreels of a stormy rescue at sea.

And now to cast my fly. I held the leader between two fingers, and the wind caught it. I lengthened the line so as to begin the swish, and the whole business slopped into the water. I picked it up and whirled it around my head—only it didn't whirl, it just clung damply to the pole. Could be I should have had a little back-yard practice, heaving a milkweed fluff into the wind with the help of a switch and a cobweb for a fishline.

I was standing there, with my banner marked Excelsior sadly drooping, when something happened with P.A. It happened in a wink, though you remember it all in slow motion. It was as though the rim of a rainbow came up out of the water, and a brownness followed, the end of P. A.'s line zigzagged through the water like a torpedo gone wild. Then that stopped too.

P. A. was reeling in his empty line. He shouted over the noise of water: "The fly was too big. He got the feather, but not the hook." Strange, but he didn't seem disappointed.

It made me feel uncomfortable. I didn't want my fish to get away—the one that was going to make Leviathan look like a guppy. And how would I handle it? I could see that juggling a greased pig would be relatively simple. I plowed upstream to where Al was working his spinner against the current. "What'll I do," I asked, "when a big fellow gets on the line?"

Looking me in the eye, he said seriously, "Only one thing to do. Stick your rod in the bank, reel him in, shinny up the pole, and choke him to death." Well, I thought, there'll be one answer to the scoffers.

Someone suddenly noticed it was 1 p.m. We marched back to the house, P. A. vigorously leading the way and I plopping along in the rear like a jalopy with flat tires. Tired and hungry . . . yet somehow the day was beautiful. Curious admission to make, for I don't usually recommend the raw, unpasteurized country air.

Meals at the Wrights' are hearty and substantial, with more coffee, more everything urged on you. Clarence usually stands in the doorway of the dining room, adding now and then to the table talk on the only subject that matters. Here's a sampling—the gist of a juicy bit of gossip—and I'm not saying who told the story, if it was told. I don't want trouble with the police, or with anglers either.

"Folks can be such liars, but what I'm telling you is true. Fellow named Burbank was one of the best fly tyers in these parts, very good for a man with a large thumb. His wife was always after him to earn a living, so finally he up and lit out to where he could find peace. But there was always the pull to come home; he recollected a big trout that he never was able to get.

*A fly fishing pupil practices under the tutelage of a sage guide in Nelson's Spring Creek. (Photograph © R. Valentine Atkinson)*

"Well, one time he did come back, and found his wife had busted up all his gear. So he smacked her once or twice, I guess with a meat cleaver. Then he run her through the meat grinder that he used for hamburgers for the trout he was raising for stock; and he took his pole—what was left of it—and a few flies and went upstream. Right in that pool, by golly, he caught the fish on a first cast. It was a beaut . . . must have been 21 inches."

At this point a man put his fork down to interrupt: "What sort of fly was he using?"

The fame of local fly tyers gave me an idea. Privately after lunch, I inquired around for the name of a man who could supply a real killer. "None better," someone said, "than Garrett Rose. You'll find him down at the railroad crossing. He's a crossing tender." I got the car and went down. Mr. Rose in his little house by the side of the railroad is certainly the friend of man. He is a large, quiet-handed, philosophical sort who knows that (theoretically) trains must run, even though fish are biting. Growing cordial at the mere mention of flies, he brought out a box with some he'd tied himself.

And again, as that first time in P. A.'s office, enthusiasm was contagious. I wanted to buy one little jewel that caught my fancy, but Mr. Rose shook his head. For right now and in these waters, he recommended a less expensive Light Cahill.

I looked at my watch. I be a black-nose dace if we hadn't been chinning for half an hour. Absorbed as we were, anything could happen, and I visioned a locomotive on its side, steam still hissing, and headlines in the paper: TRANSCONTINENTAL EXPRESS WRECKED BY A FLY. Quickly I got a couple of Cahills and hurried away, relieved that the sun was quietly shining and rails smoothly bending into uneventful vistas.

These were to be my ace-up-the-sleeve. For the present, I thought I'd try my hand at spinning. The fellows were out on the stream when I got back, with the absorbed concentration that discourages questions. I helped myself to a reel of good stout line that would hold anything up to a shark, and tied a weighted streamer to the leader with the sort of knot that would look well on a Christmas package. I worked way up above the boys (which I don't think they minded at all). My first downstream cast, outfielder-style, would have brought any fish to the surface—if it had hit him in the head.

As I was reeling in the third cast, something happened. Yessir! There was that thrill every fisherman knows when a good rod loops and promises to hold and play whatever's there. In this case, there was more hold than play. "He's sulking," I thought, advancing to the kill.

I suggest that it's never good policy to turn your back to a rushing stream when wearing waders that are just itching to float. Suddenly my feet went up and I moved downstream faster than I could reel in, ice water poured into my pants, and I got all tangled in the line. (Later I was tempted to write the manufacturer a testimonial praising his product, from which neither fish nor man can free himself once he is hooked.)

I still had a thought for my catch, and with a relatively shallow dive I brought up the rock which had found my lure irresistible. It was a beautiful four-pounder, iron-gray and sort of disk-shaped. Then I came ashore, looking like a bloated Michelin Tire man, and poured myself out of the drink.

There was somebody upstream, watching me all the while. I suppose I had a guilty conscience (spinning in the company of fly fishermen) so I casually ambled up, ready to face the music and set my soul at peace. To my surprise, it turned out to be a little lady who could be anybody's grandmother. She had on hip boots and was casting a wet fly. "You ought to be home," I said, "bending over an apple pie."

"No," she said, "pies aren't biting today." And, looking over my wet and tangled gear, "What's that clothesline for?"

I allowed I planned to use it for a leash for any stray trout I could lay my hands on, and we got to talking. She told me about how far a trout can see (maybe 35 feet in clear water) and that I shouldn't hold a fly a couple of feet above the surface, expecting the fish to jump (as she had seen me do). "He'd sooner jump into a frying pan. From down below, your fly looks like a hawk, and it puts the fish down." She fished because it taught her about fish. She explained about casting across current, and showed me the special way of tying a leader to a fly (with six twists after the loop). And then I left, feeling chastened (partly due to wet clothes which always induces in me a mood of humility).

*"First Cast of the Day!" is the exuberant title of this commissioned watercolor by Minnesota painter Bob White.*

I rejoined the fellows in time to see P. A. taking in a trout, which he netted as deftly as a poached egg. I suspected now that my course in fishing would take more than six uneasy lessons, and although I still had my Cahill to try, I began to wonder whether I'd ever catch a fish, even with a worm.

I was relieved when the sun went down.

At the house there was a young fellow named Green who had caught seven trout that day. Al kidded him, suggesting that instead of driving back with his three buddies he ought to go by bus, where there'd be a lot more people who hadn't heard about his fish. The living room filled up. Wright's place was no mere hostelry but an open house for his friends, who come back year after year to spawn their lies. Pictures of many, with their catches, adorn the walls.

Roderick Ayer and his wife dropped in. Ayer is a hearty school superintendent, who never had a rod in his hand before coming here. He uses two wet flies on his line—a Dark Hendrickson above, a Light Cahill below—and he showed photos of a dozen gleaming trophies, laid out in a row.

My cup of bitterness was complete. I longed for sleep, but even that was to be denied me. In my fevered state I sensed an undercurrent of cross purposes

between Clarence Wright and Roderick. The superintendent said that since he was moving to the Esopus (to take over a school system where the fishing is good) Clarence ought to let him have a whack at that 24-inch trout up at the pool—it was spoiled enough to be a pet and all but obstructed the stream.

Clarence said the fish was closer to 30 inches; Rod said "Let's see," and offered free of charge to bring him in before the night was over. Clarence shuddered visibly; it was like sending Billy the Kid, fully armed, to bring a young one home from school. Both Rod and Clarence have that glittering eye, and I felt that it boded no good when Rod bantered that he might go out that night and fish those posted waters, and Clarence bantered right back that he'd shoot anybody he saw, and check afterward to see if it was a friend.

"Good night, all," I said, and soon was in bed and dreaming. I dreamt I was a captive in a creel, with a big cannibal trout forcing its way through the narrow slot. I woke suddenly and sat up in a cold sweat. An explosive noise had shattered the night. It sounded as though a tire—or a school superintendent—had been punctured. I fell back into troubled sleep, wondering how many pounds Roderick would go. He had been such a nice fellow, too.

Oddly enough, I woke in the morning feeling nimble as a minnow. And there was Roderick in the kitchen, having coffee with Mrs. Wright and still chaffing Clarence. Well, that left the big fish for me!

For some reason, however, I got not a bite that day. P. A. caught another trout, which I put down to veteran's luck, and Al had several strikes, but though I fished the pool where the fabulous monster lay, he rose not to riddle, song, or dance. I went down on my knees and offered my Light Cahill. No soap. It wouldn't have surprised me if the wily patriarch had attached a note to my hook: "Go back and learn at the beginning, bub!"

Well, I was learning something fundamental as I stood in the freezing water. The stream ran as clear as jellied glycerin and with a sound like drawn silk. P. A. caught another fish; I had no hope of catching any, and I didn't mind at all. It seemed enough to be there, dipping a rod, and with every care racing away with gurgle and bubble. The art of fishing is to make fishermen.

We also fished at dusk, all of us except P. A., who had sprained an ankle. The water was a sort of fish-scale whiteness, with circles starting here and there . . . and then it happened to me too. I felt a jerk on my arm as though someone had hit the funny bone, and the rod dipped and the line caught on a rock that moved.

What does it matter that the hook came up empty? I'd had a strike on a dry fly. I was on sufferance a member of the Peerless and Benevolent Order of Fly Fishermen. Like the golf dub who knocks off a 275-foot drive, I had something to go on, build on, go bankrupt on. If the old patriarch did it just for a laugh, I shared the laugh with him. My cup of happiness was overflowing . . . or at least my waders were.

*DePuy's Spring Creek in Montana offers fly fishing in a bucolic setting. (Photograph © R. Valentine Atkinson)*

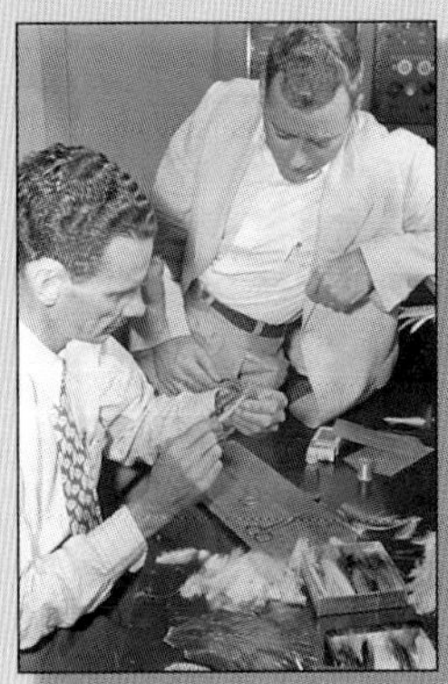

Chapter Four

# The Art of Fly-tying

"I began to tie flies. . . . A rich world of texture and color had opened to me."

*—Frank Mele, "Blue Dun"*

# “What Do You Do With All Your Spare Time?”

By Louise Dickinson Rich

Louise Dickinson Rich (1903-1991) became a best-selling author with her first book, *We Took to the Woods* (1943), which details her family's move from urban Massachusetts to the backwoods of Maine.

Unlike relative Emily Dickinson, Rich wrote to publish and earn money. The success of her first book was followed by nearly two dozen more, including the autobiographical *Happy the Land* (1946) and *My Neck of the Woods* (1950). She also authored young adult novels and books on local history, including the still popular *The Coast of Maine* (1956).

Formerly a high school English teacher, Rich left behind grading, roads, and indoor plumbing to take up country life in remote Maine—a decision questioned by many of her urbane peers. This selection from *We Took to the Woods* recounts, in Rich's simple and humorous prose, her innocent decision to try her hand at fly-tying.

PREVIOUS PAGE, MAIN IMAGE: *An angler crouches on the bank of Flat Creek, in pursuit of the wary trout. (Photograph © R. Valentine Atkinson)*

PREVIOUS PAGE, INSET IMAGE: *A pupil looks on as instructor Homer Rhode, Jr. demonstrates, in 1948, the fine art of fly-tying. (Courtesy of the Florida State Archives)*

LEFT: *An early morning angler fishes amidst sparkling waters. (Photograph © Jeff Henry/Roche Jaune Pictures, Inc.)*

THIS IS WHAT I can't decide:—whether I don't have any spare time at all, or whether most of my time is spare time. Spare time, as I used to understand it, was the time left over from doing the necessary, unpleasant things, like correcting Sophomore English themes or washing out silk stockings in the bathroom. It was the time I frittered away on useless, entertaining pursuits, like the movies or contract bridge. Now almost everything I do—except cooking—is fun, and it is also useful. There is no line of demarcation between work and play. It makes it hard to explain what I do with my spare time. . . .

About two years ago Gerrish and I took up fly tying. There were several reasons for this. We thought it would be nice to have a hobby for our evenings, for one thing. For another, flies are expensive to buy if you fish as much as we do. We're always losing flies, or having them ruined by a big fish, and it's always the fifty-cent types that meet with grief. It runs into money in the course of a season. Besides that, it was getting embarrassing for us to have to look respectful when city sports said, "Oh, of course I tie all my own flies!" as though that were a feat beyond such inept souls as we. So we took up fly tying.

I, myself, didn't intend to become a slave to the habit. I thought I'd just dabble in it, but it didn't work out that way. We were too proud to ask anyone how to go about tying flies, so we got ourselves a book of instructions and a batch of feathers and set out to teach ourselves. Gerrish gave me fair warning before we started that he couldn't learn things from books. He had to be shown; but if he could just see someone actually *do* a thing once, then he could do it all right the next time. I can follow printed directions fairly well, so the idea was that I would follow the book and Gerrish would follow me, and in that way we'd both learn. We both did, but what started out as a hobby became almost an obsession, especially with Gerrish. He's a rabid fly tyer now, and I might add, a very good one. He makes a much better fly than I do, for all that his hands are bigger and look clumsier than mine. The heads of his flies are small and smooth, while mine sometimes get beyond me and turn out large and rough. That's where the amateur betrays himself.

We thought at first that we'd be satisfied if we could make a few streamers and some of the simpler stock patterns of wet flies. We weren't going into anything complicated. We weren't even going to consider tying dry flies. We knew our own limitations. Neither of us was going to invest a lot of money in equipment. Ralph had a small vise he'd lend us, and I had nail scissors and some odds and ends of embroidery silk and yarn for bodies. There was plenty of black thread around the house, and some silver and gold string left over from Christmas wrappings, and Ralph had some beeswax in his sailmaker's outfit. He also had shellac, and we could probably find plenty of feathers and fur around the woods. All we'd have to buy was two or three dozen hooks and maybe a few feathers not indigenous to this soil, such as jungle cocks for eyes. We wouldn't have to spend more than fifty cents, all told. That's what we thought, at first.

That state of mind lasted about a month. During that month we saw everything in the light of possible fly-tying material. We brought home dead birds, and the tails of deceased flying squirrels we found, and quills out of other people's feather dusters. We clipped stiff fur from Kyak to make buck tails, and went hunting with my .22 revolver for red squirrels. (We never managed to get one.) We hounded chance acquaintances from Upton to bring us in hen feathers and hackle feathers from roosters the next time they came. And we tied up enough Plymouth Rock streamers to last us a lifetime. We had plenty of Plymouth Rock feathers, you see. Then we faced the truth. The bug had got us. We'd have to buy some more equipment—not very much, of course just a few necessary things. After all, this was partly an economy measure. We'd just spend a dollar or two.

Last spring our feather bill was over fifteen dollars. We'd already spent five or six dollars on special scissors, a pair of hackle pliers, a bottle of head varnish, a

*Water droplets gleam on an artful Fanwing Royal Coachman dry fly. (Photograph © Erwin and Peggy Bauer)*

special wax preparation, and a box of assorted hooks. Heaven knows what our bill would have been if some friends hadn't presented us with a fly-tying vise. That's what fly tying can do to you. It can make you lose all sense of proportion. We even lost our pride. When a professional fly tyer, Frank Walker, of Oxford, Maine, came to stay at Millers' that summer and offered to show us a few tricks of the trade, we forgot all about our lofty ideas of independence, and spent all one Sunday afternoon with him. He's an old man, and he's tied thousands of flies, over the course of years. He's found short cuts and practical methods that the books never dreamed of, and that it would have taken us twenty years to dope out for ourselves. And even if I never intended to tie a fly in my life, I would have enjoyed watching him work. It was really something to see him tie a Black Gnat on a No. 14 hook, with his big hands, a little stiff from rheumatism, moving slowly and delicately and surely around the almost invisible little object in the vise. Great skill and competence in any line is always impressive.

It's hard to tell exactly where the great fascination of tying flies lies. Of course, there is the satisfaction in creative work. It's fun to take a pile of raw materials and make something out of them. The more demanding the work, the greater is the satisfaction. It's fun to finish shellacking the head of a fly, hold it up, and be able to think, "There! I'll bet nobody could tell that from a bought fly!" You feel so pleased with yourself.

But that's only the beginning. People are easy to fool. The real test comes when you try the fly out on a fish. If you can catch a fish on a fly you tied yourself, then you can commence to regard yourself as a fly tyer. Still, there are always a few fool fish about that will rise to anything, so it's better to get several strikes on the fly before you indulge in too much own-back patting. But that isn't the end, either. Pretty soon you start regarding the copying of the proven, standard patterns as mere tyro's work. Anybody can copy a fly, you think. Most people know the Yellow May is good at this time of year in these waters. So there's nothing remarkable about catching a good fish on a Yellow May, no matter who tied it. Now if YOU could think up a new pattern that would catch fish, that would really be something.

So you start watching the fish. Tonight they're rising to some silvery gray little bugs that are flying up the river. If you could tie a fly that looked something like that, with perhaps a touch of yellow in the body— You reel in and go home. By working fast, you can get it done in time to try it out before dark. Perhaps it won't catch fish. All right; maybe if you used a little tinsel in the tail— There's no end to it, as you can see. And there's no feeling quite like the lift you get when eventually you hit on the right combination, and a walloping big trout comes surging up out of the shadows and grabs your very own fly, the fly you conceived and executed all by yourself.

*"One cast to the dark water and the fly vanishes. Moments later a wild rainbow splashes in the river at my feet." —Ted Leeson, The Habit of Rivers, 1994 (Photograph © Doug Stamm)*

# Hooked

By Jan Zita Grover

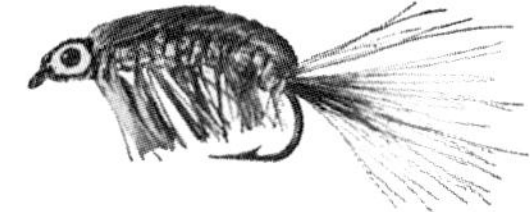

A self-taught angler, Janice Zita Grover has adopted the woods of northern Minnesota as her chosen home. Grover worked in San Francisco General Hospital during the height of the 1980s AIDS epidemic; she later sought refuge in the forests and streams of the north woods, only to find a new anguish in this area's destructive clear-cutting. Out of this experience emerged her book *North Enough: AIDS and Other Clear-Cuts* (1997), which won the Minnesota Book Award for creative nonfiction.

Grover's articles appear in publications such as *Utne Reader* and *Women's Review of Books*. She is also the author of *Silver Lining* (1983) and *Northern Waters* (1999), a collection of essays about fly fishing and the environment.

The following essay, a lyrical tribute to the physicality of fly tying, is taken from *Northern Waters*.

LEFT: *A Muddler Minnow fly. (Photograph © Doug Stamm)*

*A wondrous hat-o-flies tops the head of popular New Zealand fishing guide Simon Dickey. (Photograph © Erwin and Peggy Bauer)*

THE MORRISON IS a small dark fly noticed by Colonel Morrison upon the waters of a little lake in the Northern woods, and before observed in many other places, always eagerly seized by the trout. He preserved no specimen, but described it as a tiny black fly, having a dark red body ringed with black. The color in the body he thought was due to the blood, which in the light shone through the delicate dark skin; the wings and feet were black. The fly was made after this description. He tried it, and found it all he had hoped, and not knowing the name of the insect which it represented, allowed it to be called the Morrison.
—Mary Orvis Marbury, 1892

Even before I opened it, the package from Hunter's announced its contents by an escaping whiff of mothballs. I hefted the box: it was almost weightless, an airy reliquary of feathers rare and common, but ones that my regular hunting and gathering seldom yielded.

The package's contents took my breath away. Words don't exist for most of the colors found on a cock pheasant's skin, much less on the living bird. There are subtle, dusky teals; burnished, deep coppers; iridescent, inky greens and purples; deep, oxidized blood reds. The patterns include crescent moons, stipples, delicate scallops, chevrons. This one pheasant skin would help me construct hundreds, if not thousands, of wet flies and streamers suggestive of spiders, water striders, emergent mayflies and caddisflies, small baitfish like dace and sculpins to lure trout to my line and from thence into my supra-aqueous world.

Three nights ago, I tied for five hours. I know that because *The Jazz Image* is a three-hour show that began, ended, and was replaced by chamber music while I tied. This isn't unusual: tying is as good a way of losing track of time as fishing in a stream. Even writing that phrase, *losing track of time*, tells me that there's something woefully wrong with the way I was taught to think about nonfishing time, as if it were something to be meted out and controlled.

Tying has an unbounded quality to it—an underlying sense that time is not linear, with a past and a future, but only a now. Now I am filling the shank of this hook with a collation of animal and synthetic bits that will behave like a living being in next spring's running waters. I can see the quirky, twitchy behavior of this streamer as it eventually darts, stops, darts through the dark waters of the upper Sucker, attracting a hoard of tiny admiring brookies. Trial-and-error, plus traditional dressings, have taught me what materials will create the kind of movement I hope to impart to this streamer, what colors will translate in the dark, tannic stream into plausibly shinerlike appearance. I occupy simultaneous nows—the one of a day vividly known through all my senses on a creek and the one of my fingers working over this hook.

Dressing a fly is a ballet for fingers. They rotate, forming elegant cat's cradles, stretching and swooping around each other and the hook, stroking and ruffling materials, behaving like the flexible tools they are. Dressing a fly offers two kinds of pleasures. There's the sensuous one of watching floss flow onto the hook's shank like paint, tinsel brighten and formalize the floss, hackle produce either a fly as light and resilient as thistledown or as soft and creaturely as spider's legs. And there's also the intellectual pleasure of interpreting a living creature in dead or inorganic materials, of *building* these confections and then watching them flutter or twitch improbably to life in a dear cold stream.

The whole of my attention is focused now upon a tiny curve of steel wire somewhere between an eighth of an inch (#26) and an inch and a half (#4XL) in length. On this shank of wire, I try to create an entire, miniature world. Depending on the species of fish I am planning on presenting my fly or streamer to, the season, and the sort of water (fast or slow, clear or turbid, stream or river), I can choose to tie an imitation of a specific insect or fodder fish or an attractor whose color, size, and action in the water are designed as a general provocation.

Dressing a fly can be as simple as following the time-honored patterns in the scores of pattern books available or as complex as playing a three-dimensional chess game. I can use local samples of the various stages of invertebrate stream or streamside life as models; I can concoct fanciful attractors based on no more scientific principle than how certain colors and materials please me. Many of North America's oldest attractor flies are what were once called "lake and bass wet flies." Most of them, wrote angling historian J. Edson Leonard in 1950, "are just beautiful creations and look no more like living creatures than a traffic signal or the grille of a new Buick."

I concocted one such gaudy "fancy fly" the other night that rather pleased me: it had a red wool tag (the terminus of the body); a yellow floss body ribbed with fine oval French tinsel; a throat of red ostrich herl; a tail of iridescent green-blue peacock sword; a wing of white calf's hair, golden pheasant crest, and peacock herl surmounted by an iridescent green-black neck feather from a golden pheasant,

*"Fly Tying Legacy," a still life by Bob White, captures the hands-on quality of fly-tying.*

and a red ostrich herl collar behind its black thread head, the whole of this busy business tied onto a #8 6XL streamer hook, which is about three-quarters of an inch long.

This is the way such fancy flies were tied during their heyday, through World War II: Carrie Stevens, one of the most celebrated tiers of fancy streamers, for example, whipped up the General MacArthur during the war chiefly as a tribute (its head was wrapped in bands of red, white, and blue thread, and the feathers used to wing and hackle it were also red, white, and blue). The late fishing historian Joseph D. Bates, Jr., says of the General, "Although the fly was designed from a patriotic point of view, rather than because the colors suited accepted angling standards, the fly has proven very successful for trout and landlocked salmon in Maine waters." George and Helen Voss devised a successful streamer they named the Atom Bomb (not, as you might anticipate, consisting of melted plastics, but a standard confection of red-white-yellow-black feathers). Such gruesome whimsies will take the fish they're intended for, allowing their makers to make their cultural point and have their fish, too.

Such flies probably take brook trout readily enough, not so much because of their gaudy excesses as because the brook trout's local range is mostly bedrock streams, where the fish cannot afford to be terribly selective about what they eat. Throw fancy flies like these at brown trout, however, and you can all but hear the raspberry being blown at you through the water. But since I'm fonder of brook trout than any other salmonid, their naive avidity does not condemn them in my eyes. Rather, it offers me the license to play with fancy flies, knowing that in this case they are also practical ones.

My last concoction at 11 P.M. was another streamer for my brookies: purple floss body, silver oval tinsel rib, peacock sword tail, wing of red ostrich herl, ring-necked pheasant rump, and black dog hair, collar of golden pheasant tippet, cheeks of iridescent black starling shoulder feathers. Outside, the snow fell quietly, a Schubert oboe fantasia played on the radio, and my old wall clock ticked away all that invisible time. In the charmed circle of illumination on my cherrywood table, the soft plunder of hen necks, pheasant skins, peacock swords, flosses, tinsels, and hairs surrounded the vise and my glass of beer like the spoils of empire, which, in a sense, they were: human dominion over the rest of creation. But that wasn't how I viewed these glowing, almost indescribable feathers and hairs then: they were the relicts of life, testimony to a passing we all share, one that I am as bound up in as the creatures that passed that night through my hands, and I was inventing new lives for them, new beings compounded out of their unlikely conjunctions on tiny wire shanks. Like Mary Shelley's Doctor Frankenstein, I was inventing life, or at any rate initiating it, using the spare parts of birds and beasts otherwise cast away, twitching them into new patterns.

As I tied, it seemed as if I could see down time through all those generations of anglers and tiers who bound such hope and pleasure into their own, similar tyings. Only three generations ago, fine North American tiers prided themselves on tying without the help of vises, which they viewed as the crutches of clumsy novices. I think about that. It is like a nest of Chinese boxes, this business of tying, for each act, each material, is resonant with the long folk history of craft. Each half-hitch knot is both my particular act and one in a seemingly endless succession of knots tied not so much by individuals as by a tradition: a succession of mostly anonymous folk artists with peculiarly intimate relationships to the bodies of dead animals, mortuarists who honor the dead by recycling them.

My mind evacuated itself of all other concerns, concentrated utterly on building up a tiny mimetic world on a bit of carbon steel finer by far than the edge of a dime and in length about the span of my index fingernail. *A little world made cunningly*, if indeed I became at all good at it.

I tied off the final wind of a thread head, anointed it with a crown of clear nail polish, and surveyed my creation from all angles. Perched at the tip of the vise's jaws, it looked oddly alert and alive—a bit like a bird, an insect, a tiny fish. It glowed with the refracted light from a half dozen different beasts' and birds' coats. A fancy fly, a reliquary of history as well as of specific lives.

I turned out the light.

*Eager labs wait while their owner goes about the painstaking business of changing flies in this original Bob White painting.*

Big Body
Fly
Hook No.
New York
Ly. Amhst
Made by HARDY BROS.,
ALNWICK :: ENGLAND.
ALLCOCKS
Allcock & Co, Ltd,
SOUTH
Name
Frost & Sons
Wisconsin

# Art of Fly-tying is Set Back 2900 Years

By Red Smith

Walter Wellesley "Red" Smith (1905-1982) was a supreme sportswriter. A Green Bay native, Smith got his start with the Milwaukee *Sentinel*, but found his break at the St. Louis *Star*, where he was promoted from copyeditor to sports journalist essentially overnight.

Smith's columns have been assembled into several collections, including *Red Smith on Fishing Around the World* (1963) and *The Red Smith Reader* (1982). He won the Pulitzer Prize for Commentary in 1976 and, by the end of his career, some five hundred newspapers—both national and international—were running his daily sports column.

This article first appeared in the New York *Herald Tribune*, which syndicated his "Views of Sport" column for over twenty years. Smith imbued all his writing with personality and wit, giving equal treatment to the glorious and the mundane—from the 1951 World Series' epic "shot heard around the world," to the amateur fly tier's first Silver Tip pattern, as is related here.

LEFT: *A bass angler's gear: fly rod and reel, roomy creel, and colorful bass flies. (Photograph © Howard Lambert)*

IN CHAPTER NINE of his exhaustive treatise entitled *Flies*, J. Edson Leonard writes: "Salmon flies, which are fashioned from the plumage of the world's most beautiful and exotic birds, call for the ultimate in skill, artistic ability and color sense on the part of the fly-dresser. . . . Precedents have been so interwoven in the techniques of dressing salmon flies that even the slightest violation of any one of them is apparent to the connoisseur and, moreover, is considered intolerable by those perfectionists who demand absolute authenticity."

Mr. Leonard is not alone in this view. Fly-tying was regarded as the purest of art forms by Homer, who described the "insidious food" used for bait by Greek anglers around 1000 BC; by Claudius Aelian, who wrote at length of the flycasters on the River Astraeus in Macedonia about AD 200; by Dame Juliana Berners, prioress of the Benedictine Nunnery of Sopwell in England whose *Treatyse of Fysshynge wyth an Angle* appeared before the printing press was invented; by the sainted Izaak Walton and by all other authorities down to the great F. M. Halford in the last century.

Of the seven anglers campaigning out of this camp against Atlantic salmon, only Dick Wolters is practiced in the fly-tying art. Every night for a week he has been lashed to the wheel spinning patterns favored on the Gander River—the Black Moose, the Silver Tip, the Blue Charm, the Moose Dose.

Most of these are tied not with the plumage of exotic birds but with the beard of a deceased moose, and the stupidest grilse in the river will laugh them to scorn if they are not precisely correct down to the last turn of silk thread.

"Make me three Silver Tips and three Black Moose," demands Chuck (Camp Boss) Smith, "extra sparse, and if you ever want to fish here again make sure they don't come unraveled after three casts."

"My guide wants a thick-bodied fly," says Tom Deveaux, "with exactly six moose hairs, no more and no less. Make the body thickest in the middle."

"Thickest in the middle," says the artist. "We'll call it the Pregnant Moose. This about right?"

"That's about it," says Lester Gillingham, Deveaux's guide. "When they wouldn't touch any other fly on the river, that pattern took twenty-two salmon in four days."

"If you can find the time," says Art Smith, the fishing editor, "I'd appreciate a Cold Tip with four turns of tinsel ribbing and just a wisp of black squirrel tail."

New York anglers aware of Mr. Wolters' idiosyncrasies would be flatly incredulous.

They know that in the years he has been tying flies he has stonily refused to give, sell, lend or lease one miserable little fanwing Coachman to anybody except his grandmother, and that since she abandoned the fly rod for spinning tackle he has quit making lures for her. Yet for the first four nights here he spent so many hours toiling at the vise for others that he hadn't the time or energy to take a fish himself.

# TYING IT ALL TOGETHER

*A fly angler ruminates on a grassy Alaskan shoreline. (Photograph © Dennis Frates)*

IF YOU BECOME an avid fly angler, you go through a lot of flies. You lose them in all the typical ways.

Snagged in a bush.

Snagged on a log in the river.

Snagged in the side of that guy's neck after he tried foolishly to move into the pool you were fishing.

At about a buck and a half each, losing flies can get expensive. Eventually, most fly anglers tire of shelling out their hard-earned cash. The exception would be attorneys, who simply pad the billable hours sheet and buy more flies—which they display proudly on a patch of wool they keep on their dorsal fin and go on catching fish the usual way: in their three rows of razor-sharp teeth.

And so now we venture into one of the oldest, most traditional and enjoyable aspects of fly-fishing, a much more enjoyable way to fill our fly box. That's right, during a streamside lunch we take a handful of flies out of our friend's fly box while he's off in the bushes taking a leak.

No, actually, we begin the art of fly-tying.

And instead of *buying* flies, we create our own flies—right after we buy $200 stainless-steel vises, delicate feathers plucked from the groin area of Peruvian mountain sparrows, fur yanked from a cheetah's rump by a swift African tribesman, hooks handmade in Sweden by a man named Sven, who can, in a good week, make two of them, and fly-tying desks made of a certain type of birch that only grows on one hill in a very-hard-to-get-to part of Newfoundland.

By doing that, we will, if we live to the age of 214 and tie flies six days a week, have saved approximately forty-five cents.

*—Rich Tosches, Zipping My Fly: Moments in the Life of an American Sportsman, 2002*

At last there came a midnight when a vactioning sports writer, ashamed to beg further favors, said, "Dick, show me how to do that for myself, will you?"

Yawning, the Master tied a Silver Tip, explaining each process. "Now copy that," he said, and went to bed.

For the next half hour, his pupil fumbled with all eleven thumbs. Chances are most neophytes experience a timid little thrill of accomplishment on completing their first fly, however crude. This bungler regarded his product and fancied he could hear flapping noises, as of Walton threshing about in his grave.

The creation had a dropsical body, misshapen as the knuckles of an old baseball catcher. Some black thread had got wound over the tinsel, giving the silver tip the appearance of crooked stripes. No amount of trimming and snipping could tidy up the disheveled moose-hair wings. The eye of the hook was plastered shut with a blob of gummy black lacquer. The thing was left on the table beside the model.

Mr. Wolters rose at dawn and went fishing. When his pupil got up several hours later there was only one Silver Tip beside the vise, obviously the work of an accomplished professional. The pupil took it along and broke the barb off against a rock with a sloppy backcast.

When Mr. Wolters returned for lunch he was walking two feet above the ground, though wearing waders. He was accompanied by the bright and beautiful corpse of a salmon weighing fifteen pounds or better, the biggest taken from the Gander this season.

"What did he take?" the admiring pupil asked.

"That Silver Tip I tied just before going to bed," Mr. Wolters said. "Listen, he came out of the water when he hit and on his first long run he–"

"Er, Dick, I suppose you've got lots of Silver Tips in your fly box."

"No, just that one. It's still on the leader. Another fish took it, maybe bigger than this one, and tore loose. Listen, this fellow fought me a solid half-hour and–"

His rod, still rigged, was in the boat. On the leader was a thing with a lumpy body beginning to ravel, tattered hair wings, a tip of uneven silver and black stripes, all as neat as a Bowery flophouse.

*A gorgeous fly-caught Atlantic salmon is returned to its waters. (Photograph © R. Valentine Atkinson)*

Chapter Five

# Fly Fishing Days Gone By

"It is the ones that have got away that thrill me most, the ones that keep fresh in my memory."

–Ray Bergman, *Trout*

# *In Pursuit of Bass*

*By Joan Salvato Wulff*

Joan Salvato Wulff won her first casting title in 1938. The same year, she started ballet and tap dancing lessons. Two years later, Wulff was teaching dance and traveling to regional casting tournaments. She was thirteen years old.

A precocious child and a fearless women, Wulff is a legend in the fly fishing world. With the income she earned running a dance school, she funded her travels to casting tournaments and, competing largely against men, won seventeen national and one international casting titles.

"I loved fly casting because of the grace and beauty of it," says Wulff. Distance casting particularly entrances her, and in 1960, she broke the women's record by casting a fly line a remarkable 161 feet.

The first fishing columnist for *Fly Rod & Reel* magazine, Wulff has written three books on fly fishing technique, including *Joan Wulff's Fly Fishing: Expert Advice from a Woman's Perspective* (1991), from which the following nostalgic reminiscence is taken.

PREVIOUS PAGE, MAIN IMAGE: *An angler heads upstream in this peaceful watercolor painting by Canadian painter Richard Vander Meer.*

PREVIOUS PAGE, INSET IMAGE: *This undated photograph depicts a no-frills fishing camp from the past. These anglers are headed to Mohawk Lake in the Breckenridge area. (Courtesy of the Colorado Historical Society)*

LEFT: *A hooked largemouth bass explodes out of the water. (Photograph © Doug Stamm)*

*Father and daughter pause to check their fly. (Photograph © Doug Stamm)*

FLY-ROD BASS FISHING is the genesis of my being a fisherman, as I related in the Introduction. My dad loved it. Mom didn't fish, so she rowed the boat. From that evening in the early 1930s when my child's mind formed the thought "It is better to be the fisherman than the rower," I shared that love with my late dad.

I have fished with surface flies for largemouth and smallmouth bass in ponds, lakes, reservoirs, canals, and quarry pits in the South and as far north as Ontario. Bass are also caught on underwater flies and found in moving water, but my preference is for still water and the chance of bringing them to the surface. Over the years, I've cast from various boat "platforms," ranging from wooden rowboats to the current custom-designed bass boats that are made of fiberglass. These are carpeted and boast elevated bucket seats and an electric trolling motor pedal that sits right under your foot.

Although it is easy to get used to motorized "rowing," it is my unfulfilled dream to have my own leaky wooden rowboat on a lake somewhere nearby, into which I can jump on a summer's evening to spend a couple of hours lazing along in pursuit of bass.

Wooden—and leaky—will give me the nice, slow speed I want in covering water. One pull on the oars and I'll be able to make three or four presentations to likely bass cover without any feeling of "hurry up, before you've passed this place" as I would experience in a boat with an electric motor. I want it like it used to be.

The aura of bass fishing is one of complete relaxation with a hint of excitement to come. Bass are unpredictable, aggressive, and scrappy. Some anglers believe that inch for inch and pound for pound, bass are the gamest fish that swim. Smallmouths are more likely to fit that description than are largemouths, but for me it is the anticipation of the strike, of either species, on a surface bass bug that holds the most intrigue.

*A solitary angler plies the quiet, misty waters of Leigh Lake in Grand Teton National Park. (Photograph © Erwin and Peggy Bauer)*

Bass burst through the water's surface so explosively that a natural bait would surely die of a heart attack. I prefer not to see them coming to the fly, so that it is a complete surprise, compounded by the anticipation built up beforehand. Let me tell you what it's like.

A summer evening. A quiet lake; no dwellings. Lily pads and sunken logs, frogs croaking to each other, blackbirds flitting among the cattails before it gets dark. A mosquito hums and goes by. The moon starts up over the nearby hill. The creek of the oars and the sounds of the fly line and bass bug swishing through the air are all you can hear as the frogs suddenly fall silent. The deer-hair bug lands with a plop in an opening in the lily pads. Silence descends again as I wait for all of the ripples to disappear from the surface—like Dad used to do it. It seemed so long to wait, back then.

But not now. I'm anticipating. It's time for one twitch of the bug. The fly line is under my rod hand and when I have drawn all the slack out of it, I give it a sudden pull through the water and *pow!* a largemouth erupts from the water to take the fly. It keeps climbing upward with the fly still not set in its mouth and then lands with a loud *splat.* I strike to set the hook, but it is too late, the fly is mine again. I missed.

Now I am again aware of the frogs. The rowboat moves slowly along the shore and the glow of the low-hung moon adds mystery to the surroundings. The lily pads end temporarily and a half-sunken log is the next likely cover to explore. My first cast goes between the pads and the log. This time, after waiting for the ripples to disappear, I move the bug rather rapidly back toward the boat, using the line strip method with the rod tip low to chug it. I'm full of anticipation again. There is no action, but perhaps the disturbance woke somebody up!

My next cast goes to the same place and my tactics are the same until I get near the log, and then I dead-stop the bug. And twitch it. Anticipation. Another twitch. Nothing; just anticipation. I twitch it and stop it all the way back to the boat. No bass seems to care.

A tiny pull on the oars lets me put the next cast on the far side of the log and go back to my first tactic, waiting for the ripples to disappear before I make the rapid chugging retrieve. But I never get the chance to retrieve it, and this time I am *not* anticipating the explosion as the dark and deep-bodied outline of a hungry largemouth bass engulfs my fly. As he turns downward, I set the hook and he dives, only to come up a few seconds later in a beautiful moonlit leap, shaking his head from side to side as he tries to get rid of the fly. I move the rod in unison with his moves, creating a little tension so he won't get purchase on the bulky bug.

As he falls back into the water, I take the advantage and put pressure on him to keep him from wrapping the line or leader around the log. I move him toward the boat, but he suddenly surges under it, taking line. I let him go, leaning over the side and stabbing the water with my rod for half its length to keep in touch. I work my rod around the boat and come up on the other side, the open-water side, waiting again for the least sign of his slowing down. He jumps and then jumps again. I take the advantage once more as he crashes back into the water. With a low sideward angle on the rod I pressure him toward where I sit and then raise the rod to slide him next to the boat, taking him by surprise.

Quickly, I reach down and grip him by his lower jaw with my thumb in his mouth, his large mouth I might add, and lift him from the water to admire. He remains quiet (the grip has this effect) while I back out the fly. I thank him for giving me the chance to see him in action, and I think about the next angler who'll have the same thrill as I head him back toward his log cover, none the worse for wear.

Heading back to the boat landing, I wear a big smile on my face that reaches through my whole body.

*A smallmouth bass goes in pursuit of a fly in this lifelike work by Toronto artist Charles Weiss. Weiss, who specializes in wildlife paintings and illustrations, says, "My favorite subjects are dramatic underwater situations."*

# *Upon the Earth Below*

*By Gordon MacQuarrie*

Gordon MacQuarrie (1900–1956) got his start as a cub reporter with the Superior, Wisconsin, *Evening Telegram*. A talented writer, he easily climbed the ranks to managing editor. Nationally, newspapers and sporting magazines snapped up MacQuarrie's witty tales of hunting and fishing, and in 1936, he became America's first outdoors editor. A true storyteller with a masterful command over mood and character, MacQuarrie held this coveted position with the Milwaukee *Journal* for twenty years.

MacQuarrie is best known for inventing the beloved Old Duck Hunters' Association, led by one Mister President—a curmudgeonly character inspired by his father-in-law. These tales have been collected in the timeless trilogy, *Stories of the Old Duck Hunters*, *More Stories of the Old Duck Hunters*, and *Last Stories of the Old Duck Hunters*.

This story, an early installment in the famed Duck Hunters series, calls to mind the archetypal pair of schoolboys who must throw a few punches to become lifelong friends—only here they compete with fly rods, not fists.

LEFT: *Autumn brings anglers in search of salmon and steelhead to the North Umpqua River. (Photograph © Dennis Frates)*

THERE IS SOMETHING about rain. . . . At night in summer when the clouds can swell no more and shrink from threatening battlements to ragged shreds over Wisconsin, I often get up from my chair, go to the big closet and speculate over the implements of trout fishing there. Indeed, there is something about rain. Especially a warm rain, spilled over a city or a network of trout streams. It kindles a spark. It presses a button. It is an urgent message from afar to any seeker of the holy grail of anglingdom—trout.

There is the mild August rain sluicing down to the thirsty earth. There are the castellated clouds, fresh from the Western prairie, borne on the hot, dry land wind. And there is your man of the creel and the throbbing rod and the sodden waders going to the window to peer out and plumb the mysteries of the rain and wonder about tomorrow.

It must be that aeons ago, when the rain splashed down over the front of a cave door, the muscle-bound troglodyte within went to the opening and stretched out his hand, palm upward. Perhaps he even stood in it a bit, as perfectly sane men will sometimes do. Perhaps that old sprig of Adam, restless by his fire in the dry cave, felt the friendliness of the rain. Perhaps—no troutster will deny it—he felt the drops upon his matted head and wondered about tomorrow.

*A brown trout measures out impressively against the angler's fly rod and net. (Photograph © R. Valentine Atkinson)*

The rain can beckon a man of the noisy city and draw him to the door or window. Its attraction is so much the greater if it falls at night, when it is a whispering mystic visitor from afar that seems to say: "Get ready, my friend. I am just brushing by to settle the dust and wash away today's dead spent-wings"

One night I was sitting alone, restless behind my newspaper. The rain had barely begun. I was feeling its pull. Dark had just fallen, and the rain had come tentatively, like a guest afraid of a cool welcome. It had grown darker, and the rain came stronger. I cast the paper aside and went to the door.

All of the lush buoyance of August was in the night wind that came through the screen. To my nostrils came the scent of wet turf, and in the sparkling lines of rain that penciled down in the porch light I seemed to see the exuberant waters where the trout dwell.

I stared out. The lightning flashed on and off. Two pine trees by my door tossed and glistened. I was lost there for minutes contemplating the beauty of the night.

Also, I knew what the rain would do for certain trout waters. Some of them it would raise; some would even go over their banks. Others, mothered by heavily grown forest country, would take up the water slowly. The trout would be grateful, as it had been dry and hot for a long time. There would be new feed in the streams tomorrow.

*Anglers pole a canoe down the scenic Brule River in this original painting by Bob White.*

From my dry vestibule, nose pressed to the screen, over which hung a small protecting porch roof, I made out, in one lightning flash, the figure of a man. He was walking slowly and deliberately in the downpour. He came across the street under the corner light, and at the distance of fifty yards I could see that the water had flattened the brim of his hat.

He vanished into darkness, walking toward me. Here, I said, is a man doing what I would wish to do if I didn't give a rip about the crease in these trousers. A man out shaking hands with an August rainstorm. I enjoyed his enjoyment. I could almost feel the warm drops cascading off my nose, the squishing of my shoes and the cool touch of rain on my cheeks.

He came closer, passing the mountain ash trees near my walk, sloshing as slowly and happily as ever. And then, as though he had seen me, he turned up my walk. It was not until he strode into the wan light of the tiny porch that I recognized him—the President of the Old Duck Hunters' Association.

He stood beyond the porch roof in the drip, grinning in at me. "This is it," he said.

"And you're fixing to catch a dandy summer cold. Come in."

He stamped off some of the drops, dashed the water from his soaking hat and sized me up. "A little rain," he lectured, "never hurt anyone. Especially a fisherman. This is exactly what these August trout streams have been waiting for."

I lured him inside.

"How about tomorrow?" he said.

I was not given an opportunity to accept his invitation. He rushed on.

*A fisherman turns to his fly box for inspiration on a Montana river. (Photograph © R. Valentine Atkinson)*

"It's close to the end of the month now. This will be the last warm rain of the season. Next good one we get will be a cold September drizzle. Wait and see. Better get that trout fishin' done while there's time. A trout has got to have new rain every so often. . . ."

In the living room the situation hit me differently. The spell of the storm had left me, and now all I could think of was Mister President, dripping on my newly covered davenport, selling me a bill of fishing goods. I laughed. It must have seemed a smug laugh to him, such a laugh as a nonventuresome, dry-shod city prisoner would get off in the presence of a dyed-in-the-wool trout fisherman.

"Laugh and be danged," he snorted. "I'll walk five more blocks in this very fine rainstorm to the door of a real fisherman, and I'll bet you anything he'll not only come along with me tomorrow, but he'll walk home with me in the rain—without an umbrella."

I capitulated, of course. It is always good wisdom to capitulate to a President of the Old Duck Hunters. I even offered him dry socks and a hot drink and spread his dripping jacket in front of the gas oven. He sat there for a long spell, talking trout, and when his warming drink was finished he strode back into the night, to walk like a man and a trout fisherman in the friendly element.

It was not until the next afternoon that I plumbed his further thoughts about the rain. I wanted to get the whole of his philosophy of tramping through a downpour. I sensed a little of it, but wanted to learn more of what stirs the depths of such as he.

"It's like this," he said, shifting his cigar and leaning over the steering wheel which was guiding us to the Iron River, in north Wisconsin. "Up to yesterday it hadn't rained in weeks. I was getting as dry as your hollyhocks. Every day had been the same. Bright, dazzling sun, same old grind in the office. Monotony.

"Then it rained. I was working late. I watched that storm gather, and the heavier the clouds came in from the west the better I felt. Do you suppose there's anything to this here theory that a little electricity in the air peps up a fellow? I kept working through the rain, getting more done than I had all day. And when I was through I said, 'Now for a good walk in the rain.' Why? I just wanted to. The reason I came to your house first was so I could dry off some before my wife saw me."

I didn't quite get it yet.

He continued: "Don't you ever feel like plunging into a snowstorm, or wading a tough river, or climbing a hill? Maybe it's a way of letting off steam. Or maybe I've fished trout so long I'm getting just like a trout, rushing out from under the bank in a rain to see what the river is bringing down for supper. Could be."

I looked him over. A lean, keen business man, much like many another business man except for the fisherman's garb. Sharp brown eyes, a mouth on the upturned quizzical side, horn-rimmed glasses, a goodly swath of gray in the black hair. Yes, he might have been any other harassed slave of commerce on a fishing recess, but he was not. There was something of the boy about him which most men pretend to outgrow, and, doing so, thus become old.

*A cold winter's day doesn't stop this angler from fly fishing Oregon's Chewaucan River. (Photograph © Dennis Frates)*

We drove to the Iron in bright sun, and the President stuffed his faded khaki fishing jacket with the things he would need. He donned waders, rigged up, applied mosquito dope, and, with a final flourish, adjusted the old brown fishing felt with the hook-marred band. Then he was gone, leaving me to climb into gear and ruminate upon a way of life that brings a man to an even three-score with the heart of a boy.

I got into the Iron at a little meadow-like spot not far from Wisconsin's Highway 13. The sun was high. Last night's rain had hardly raised the stream. There was a freshness in the woods that all trout fishermen will recall—the freshness of soaking turf and rain-washed air, and the silver tinkling of a wren and the sweet lament of a white-throated sparrow. I hardly feel that I have been trout fishing if I do not hear this precious bird along the stream.

Things went indifferently for an hour. Fish were rising, but they were the tiny, ubiquitous rainbows, so common in streams that empty into Lake Superior and so laughably pugnacious, coming out to smash a fly like a feather-weight sparring with Joe Louis.

By four o'clock the outdoor stage was being set as it was the previous evening. The black, bulbous clouds in the west, borne into Wisconsin by the day-long prairie wind, were rumbling and flickering distantly. I knew it was only a matter of minutes before the storm would be over the Iron.

But it was a fine time to fish. As the first drops fell I got into a fair rainbow, creeled it and went on hastily, to search other likely corners. From a grassy place in midstream came a big enough brown, enticed out of its scant cover by the lure of new food. Downstream a bit I took two more rainbows. All came to a very, very wet single Royal Coachman.

A wind came out of those plumbeous clouds that stirred the popples joyously, so that their long-stemmed leaves turned upward and revealed the silver gray of their under sides. I could feel the rain going through canvas and flannel to my shoulders. The river was boiling like a kettle. "Fine," said I. Trout were out in it.

The President was out in it. I was out in it. Let it come. I looked back, and there, a hundred yards downstream, was the President, hailing me.

"Hurry up!" he yelled.

I went to him. He was certainly in a hurry. He had his rod taken down, but the line was still strung through the guides. "Got to get out of here quick," he said. He was short of breath. He had hurried to locate me.

"Get out of here?"

"And I mean right now—clay roads!"

I hadn't thought of that. I got to the car ahead of him. I was remembering stalled cars in Lake Superior's red clay and one nightmare exit from a similar spot where he and I made it out only by wrapping wool socks around the wheels in lieu of chains.

*A fly fisherman's dream: a fly hatch and a solitary stretch of river. (Photograph © Jeff Henry/Roche Jaune Pictures, Inc.)*

No time to climb out of waders. The rain was sluicing down. We had one chance of getting out of that clay-road country to graveled highway. It lay in the fact that we would be the first ones over the sharply crowned road on which we had come in. We might, by luck and careful driving, bite down with our tires and get hold of traction.

It was nip and tuck. But we made it, thanks to the skillful tooling of Mister President, who is an old hand with slippery clay roads. There were a couple of little hogbacks, however, that we actually slid down.

On the graveled road, he drew up at the side and switched off the motor. It was around 4:30 by then. He pawed around in the back seat and came up with sandwiches and coffee. Studying the rain-dashed windshield, he made more trout medicine.

"We'll go back to the Brule, in by George Yale's at Rainbow Bend, and have one more fling at it. Won't have to worry about roads there."

Further trout fishing had been far from my mind, but just when you think the President is in a corner he wriggles out and starts a new campaign. "No hurry," he pointed out. "Sit there and finish your coffee—and here, sit on this old raincoat. I can't have you ruining the upholstery on a new $1,800 automobile."

Ruin the upholstery! Heck, I had been with him in the scrub-oak country one day when those tough-tipped branches made an $1,800 job look as if it had been sandpapered. He wasn't concerned. He was more concerned about two limits of mallards we had taken that day from a hard-to-get-at pot-hole.

"About seven o'clock will be soon enough to hit the Brule," he ventured. "Just a half hour or hour is all I want. A few good ones ought to be out by then."

We sat and talked. We even had time, between showers, to straighten out some of our hastily stowed tackle, and the heat of our bodies partially dried our upper clothing. We talked as do all trout fishermen confined in an auto—of politics and making money and how to get along with one's neighbors and fishing for trout and waiting in frosty duck blinds at dawn.

Fed and reorganized, we drove slowly south and a bit west to the Brule at Rainbow Bend. It is a favorite putting-in place for the confirmed wader. On the peak of land which juts out into this enticing stream in front of the forest ranger's house we sat for more minutes and watched the sun go down behind threatening clouds. By then it had stopped raining. The President lit a fresh cigar and studied the clouds from the west.

"It'll rain again," he predicted.

Darkness was coming fast. The woods dripped. A few between-the-rain mosquitoes were venturing forth. A whippoorwill sent out an exploratory note.

"What time shall we meet at the car?"

"I don't like this fishing in the dark myself," he explained. "Let's fish for an hour and call it a day."

At this place, where the pines lean over the Brule, he jointed his rod and was off down the path on the right bank. I put in above the Ranger's station, intending to fish above the old stone dam in a stretch that I respect most highly for its combination of quite fast water and long, deep holes. In late summer when aerated water is preferred by trout, I have found this place to be excellent.

Such evenings are long remembered. Nighthawks swooped and cried above me as I went slowly upstream on the right bank. Before I got to my beginning point my neck and shoulders were soaked again from dripping trees.

*Western photographer Frank Jay Haynes (1853-1921) captured this quintessential trout fishing image in 1896. Famous for his photography of Yellowstone National Park, Haynes sold his images to tourists from a studio at Mammoth Hot Springs. (Courtesy of the Haynes Foundation Collection, Montana Historical Society)*

It was still light enough to hold the eye of a fly to the graying sky and thread a 1X leader through it. I like thus place. I have been very lucky here. I leaned against a great rock while I tied on a floater and studied for the hundredth time the familiar stairway of rapids which lay before me.

One of the best things about trout fishing is going back to a familiar place. Then the woods welcome a man. It is not like being alone on a strange river.

I worked out line over the wavelets at the foot of my rapids, but turned over nothing more than the omnipresent baby rainbows. Hugging the right bank and working farther into the hard flow of this swift water, I did better across in the slack water of the left bank when an 11-inch brown, tempted by a back-circling bivisible in an eddy, smacked it hard and sure.

Very well. They were out on the prod, following the rain as Mister President had judged they would be. They seemed everywhere in that foaming water. And they were not choosy. It was dark enough to invite them to be impetuous, and light enough to make for agreeable fishing.

The fish of that place I remember was a stout brown. It came out of the swiftest water in mid-current, seized the fly and went downstream, all in one swoop. With a four-ounce rod and a 1X leader in that kind of water a solid fish like this

*An angler wades into Yellowstone Lake on a soft autumn morning. Legend has it the rocks lining this stretch of the north shore are part of an ancient Native American fish trap. (Photograph © Jeff Henry/Roche Jaune Pictures, Inc.)*

one, below a man, has all the advantage. I stumbled downstream after him, played him out in the slack water and slipped him in the rubber pocket of my jacket. I thought then that he might go 18 inches. Anyway, I decided, I would claim that length before Mister President.

By squinting a bit I made out the time—8:30. The hour was up. I returned to the car in the pines on the hill, put everything carefully away, examined the buster trout gloatingly in the car headlights and composed myself behind the wheel to wait for Mister President. Off in the west there was hardly enough daylight remaining to backlight the pointed spruce tops. Back of me and over me the sky was invisible. A big drop of rain hit the windshield hard. I sensed what was coming.

*Water droplets fly as a rainbow trout tries to shake loose a Royal Coachman. (Photograph © Doug Stamm)*

There was a pause in the small night sounds of the Brule valley. I listened. From far off came the bold, surging roar of rain on leaves. The sound came nearer, rushing through the woods in an ear-filling crescendo. Then the rain hit.

It made a goodly cascade on the windshield. It hammered at the steel car top. It was a million wet drumsticks on the hood. With it came a wild, quick wind, whooping and screaming through the tree-tops. The lights, switched on, revealed steel-bright pencils of rain.

Too bad. The President was down in that rain-stricken valley somewhere getting soaked anew. He might have escaped a second wetting had he quit the stream at the appointed time. He might have been sitting there with me in the dry front seat, looking out into it.

I was feeling pretty smug about it. The President is a late-stayer. This time, I thought, he was going to pay the penalty for not keeping an appointment. And then there was that damp, comforting lump in the rubber-lined pocket. I could feel it by reaching a hand down over the back of the seat to where my jacket lay on the floor.

I would take my time about showing him that one. I'd be nonchalant. I'd haul out the little ones first, wait for him to snort at them and then produce the good one. I'd show him. I'd say it was a wonder a man can't depend on his best friend's word. I'd say that when I tell a fellow I'll meet him at such and such a time I meet him then, and don't keep him waiting in a cloudburst.

Time dragged. I am an impatient waiter. Would he ever return? A half hour passed. Then an hour. I turned on the lights from time to time at imaginary sounds from the path up which he would come. It was a long, boring, fretful wait.

Just after the legal quitting time of 10 P.M., I really did hear boots crunch against gravel. I switched the lights on to light his way, for it was Mister President. He came forward in the downpour. The old brown felt was sagging. He wore that unconcerned, listless air of a fisherman who is about to declare, "I gave 'em everything in the book, but they wouldn't play." I opened the car door, and he squished in. Played out, he demanded hot coffee and sipped it while listening to my evening's report.

He lighted up some at the sight of the 18-incher, but said it wouldn't go more than 15. "Maybe only 14½," he ventured. Nope, he hadn't a thing worth while. That dratted rain! And when it grew dark, he had his troubles in fighting the river without a flashlight. He wormed out of wet gear and into dry, gol-durning his luck and the weather. We prepared to drive home.

*A hardy winter fly fisher braves the frigid waters of the Snake River in search of whitefish. (Photograph © Erwin and Peggy Bauer)*

"I'll take down your rod," I offered, and went outside to where he had leaned it against a fender.

I hastily disjointed it and crawled back behind the wheel, handing the rod joints back to him. Then I discovered I was sitting on something. Something big and cold and wet. Something he had put in my place while I was getting the rod.

I turned around and stared down at the largest just-caught native brook trout I have seen come out of the Brule. Later it went a mite under four pounds—something of a miracle in this day and age, when all men know the big fish of the Brule are invariably browns or rainbows.

Hizzoner was chuckling now. The fish, he explained, hit a No. 4 brown fly that didn't have a name. He had heard it feeding in the dark and rain, and stayed with it for a half hour until it rose to the fly. He admitted it was the largest brookie he had ever taken in the Brule.

I stared at it as a man will stare at so rare a treasure. I envisioned the battle that took place down in that storm-lashed valley. The lightning must have seen a classic combat that night. I held the fish up and examined it by the dome light. "How long do you suppose it is?"

He snorted a triumphant snort from his throne in the rear and shot back: "Put it alongside that 18-incher of yours. The way you figger, it'll go just a yard long—just one yard!"

# No Wind in the Willows

*By Russell Chatham*

Russell Chatham writes and paints from his home in Livingston, Montana. His landscape lithographs hang on the walls of national and international galleries, as well as the homes of private collectors such as Thomas McGuane, Hunter S. Thompson, Angelica Huston, and William Randolph Hearst III.

Chatham's paintings exhibit a melancholy beauty, as does his prose. He publishes stories and essays in magazines from *Fly Rod & Reel* to *The Atlantic*. He also has two collections, *The Angler's Coast* (1976) and *Dark Waters* (1988), which are available through Chatham's publishing house, Clark City Press.

Chatham's writing has been described as opinionated and ornery; it has also been termed bold, sensual, and full of decency. It's all true. Chatham is simply one of the most honest and excellent contemporary writers you'll come across.

This essay from *The Angler's Coast* is peopled with policemen, a convict, and millions of San Francisco commuters. The joy is in watching Chatham make it beautiful.

LEFT: *A school of striped bass glide through coastal waters. (Photograph © Doug Stamm)*

OUTSIDE A BLIZZARD is raging, and the familiar edges that normally define my yard, with its fences, woodpile, and barns, have long vanished beneath the snow. My house, the last on an unpaved road among aspen and pine forests along the northwestern perimeter of Montana's vast Absaroka wilderness, is well on its way toward becoming a smallish speck on the surface of a preposterous marshmallow.

I'm unable to go out, and as I sit in my kitchen, staring out the window, a word recurs, an idea, insisting itself upon the situation: remoteness. I moved to Big Sky country to get it. As an angler reflecting upon the fabric of American sport afield, I recognized the essential thread to be a romance with far places. In short, I'd identified the Mainstream and wanted in.

*"Once more the magic bend and flex of a well-designed rod."*
*—W. D. Wetherell, One River More, 1998 (Photograph © Doug Stamm)*

My early fishing days were spent in a northern California cabin snuggled against the hillside beneath stands of redwood. Fishing was more plain and intimate then, and the invocation "Take a boy fishing!" required but a few Bass-O-Renos and perhaps a small outboard motor, called a "kicker," for immediate implementation. On a bookshelf beside our cabin's fireplace was a pile of old magazines, sporting journals mostly, and some outdated tackle catalogues. This collection of allusions was rife with visions of adventure in which the canoe loomed large as a vehicle of escape. A guide, invariably of French descent and dressed appropriately in a red-and-black-checked wool shirt, took us to lakes and rivers teeming with unusually large brook trout or northern pike somewhere in the vastness of the Canadian outback. *Portage!* How much more a vision of unsoiled landscape this word promised than, say, ecology.

But before I founder completely in fatuous recall, it occurs to me that until very recently, among the hundred thousand-odd words placed by the *Oxford Unabridged* at my disposal, the adjective least correct to describe my own angling past is remote.

San Francisco Bay: It is four-thirty in the morning on June 21, 1966. I am later than planned because of the time it took to clear myself with the policeman who pulled me over in San Anselmo for "suspicious behavior." Was it the generally fishy odor about the car which, in the end, convinced the law of my salient innocence? I don't know. In any case, we parted amicably.

*An angler proudly displays a bluegill caught on a fly rod. (Photograph © Doug Stamm)*

Now I am parking the car near a maintenance station on the Marin County end of the Richmond-San Rafael Bridge. I expect to be joined soon by an acquaintance but since he hasn't arrived I decide to walk out to the bridge itself for a quick preview. On the way, rats scurry for cover behind a shabby row of shrubs. These would not be your large Norways, the kind you might see in the tropics sitting boldly in a palm while you sip your rum and tonic on the veranda below. No, the pusillanimous little rodents that people my morning are inclined to cower behind slimy rocks near the freeway, struggling on an equal footing with Marfak for control of the last strands of seaweed, or waiting in crevices for the next colloidal high tide.

I brush past the *Pedestrians Prohibited* sign, jump the low guardrail, and trot to the second lightpost. There is no visible traffic but from the north I hear a diesel truck shift down just before the crest that will bring him into view and then onto the bridge approach. He will be doing seventy when he reaches me so I hook one leg over the railing, grip the light standard, and try to become inconspicuous. I would rather not be sucked under the rear wheels of a truck and trailer full of rutabagas. He goes by with a blast and the bridge vibrates ominously as I watch his lights fade toward Richmond.

I run out to the next light and look down. As I'd hoped, half a dozen dark forms are finning in the shadow beneath the bridge. I am especially excited by the largest, which is a striped bass of at least thirty pounds. To my right, a pod of smelt moves nearby on a tangent certain to prompt an attack. The little fish are attracted by the brilliant light overhead. In their lack of purpose they seem ephemeral, like a translucent curtain quivering near a window, while the heavy predators lurking in the dark are deliberate and potent. In a moment the black shapes explode outward, sending the smelt arcing away in a shower of flashing bodies.

Satisfied, I turn back toward the approach in time to see the California Highway Patrol car coming at me, its nose down under heavy braking.

"What are you doing out here, buddy?"

"Going fishing soon as it's legal time."

"Is that your car parked back at the maintenance building?"

"Yes."

"Well, it's illegally parked. Better move it. Now get going and don't walk out here anymore."

On my way to the car I see the patrolman who'd questioned me get out and look over the railing. Then the amber light is flashing and the driver is out too. Together they lean over the side, pointing.

I see Frank's blue sedan come down the exit ramp and turn south. When I reach him he is untying his boat and I begin to do the same. In a few seconds we will have them in the water. In order to launch we must trespass. The land belongs to the State of California, and although I've never been verbally warned off, any number of *Keep Out* signs are posted.

*A summer angler releases his quarry in this richly toned painting by artist Richard Vander Meer.*

For about eight years I kept a boat chained and locked behind a large sign reading *Cable Crossing*. Once a year the sign would be repainted, and white paint would get on the chain. Some yards away in a square blockhouse belonging to San Quentin Penitentiary, trustees worked during the day. Each season they planted a handsome little vegetable garden which I was careful never to disturb. I often talked to one convict in particular after fishing. It would take some minutes to put the boat behind the sign and then carry everything else up to the car. He would call a greeting and I'd perhaps comment on the progress in the garden. Then he'd ask, always rather plaintively, about the fishing. He said he'd liked to go fishing before he got "inside."

One December we had a severe storm, accompanied by especially high tides. Afterward, I went over to check the boat and all that was left was the chain. I was poking around the beach when I heard my friend's voice.

"Looking for your boat?"

"Guess it's gone," I replied sadly.

"No, I saw it break loose and caught it. Then I dragged it up there," he said. "Only thing I couldn't find was the seat." Beyond the garden I could see the trim little El Toro upside down on a pair of two-by-fours.

In recent years there have been no inmates at the blockhouse and the garden lies fallow beneath wild anise. In a sense this has meant more license to trespass but I stopped keeping a boat behind the sign when I knew there would be no trustees to look after it.

*Maxwell House uses fly fishing in this 1946 advertisement to evoke "the American Scene." Illustrated with a classic Adolf Dehn watercolor, this ad appeared in Life magazine.*

Back at the launch, it is a windless, overcast morning. Sunrise is due in an hour but the eastern horizon over San Pablo Bay is still dark. Bursts of flame glow against a cloudy ceiling above Point Molate, tangible evidence that behind the Tatter's headlands lies the Standard Oil Company of California's research center. Its sprawl of cylinders, cones, and rectangles is petroleum's bitter ode to the cubists. At Point San Quentin, the flaring fires have become a familiar greeting, like the dew on a chokecherry bush that starts off the trout fisherman's day in the Rockies.

"Did you look?" Frank asks.

"They're there."

We row around the tilted bow of a derelict tugboat, then past rotted pilings left from the ferryboat days. Over on the approach a yellow bridge-patrol truck moves slowly, flashing its warning lights. Switching on a spotlight, the driver scans the water, catching sight of Frank and me. Then the light is off and the truck starts toward the toll plaza. Unseen overhead, a black-crowned nighthawk rasps its singularly forlorn call. The smell of an institutional breakfast wafts unappetizingly across the water from San Quentin, an odor not unlike that of a cow barn in winter. No croissants and chilled grapefruit sections this morning, to be sure.

There is a fast tide and we must row smartly to pass beneath the bridge, where it is always dank and dripping. Sounds are magnified and echoed, especially the wavelets slapping against pilings. Reflected light plays on the girders overhead, and just before we emerge I see several bass hovering at the edge. Frank rows into the dark while I decide to try a few casts at the first light. The piling directly beneath the lamp attracts my attention so I drop the large bucktail fly where the current will swing it into the shadows.

*A successful day's brook trout fishing is depicted in this 1862 Currier & Ives lithograph.*

Instantly there is a take and I set the hook twice. This is always the moment when I wonder if the bass will go under the bridge and break off on a sharp barnacle. But I've learned that initial light pressure generally encourages them to dive toward the boat. Now my bass pulls around into the dark, and I try to gauge its size. It is a stubborn fish that resolutely resists all the strain I can manage on a fifteen-pound tippet. Eventually I land it and estimate a weight slightly above twenty pounds. Frank is anchored under the third light, where I see angular splashes as fish erupt under a school of bait.

Walt Mullen showed me the bridge and how to fish it. When we first met, shortly after it was built, I was sixteen and he was more than eighty. Walt had taken my father fishing and hunting back in the twenties when my dad was going to Stanford.

Mullen was an old sign painter, wiry and spry, surely no more than a hundred pounds soaking wet. I wanted to learn the sign business so I hung around his shop. Because my patience proved short and my business acumen entirely nonexistent, we always ended up talking about fishing. He loved it more than anyone I'd ever met. In the front pocket of his coveralls he always had a tide book, dog-eared and paint-smeared.

"See here," he said one day, pointing out the numerals. "There's a good tide in three days. If the water's clear and it's not too windy, I'll take you out to the bridge."

At that point my own experience was primarily academic insofar as fly-casting for striped bass was concerned. Walt didn't fly-fish but he knew instinctively I would catch fish on the streamers I showed him. I'd read about certain pioneer anglers on the East Coast who caught striped bass by fly-fishing. I knew also that Joe Brooks, the noted Virginian, was much interested in stripers and had caught one of twenty-nine pounds, six ounces in 1948 out of Coos Bay, Oregon. This fish was the acknowledged fly-rod record.

For several years Walt and I fished together regularly, until I married and became too busy and he closed his shop, moving the business to another county. Occasionally I'd see him at the bridge. His eyes were failing and he didn't trust himself in a boat anymore, so he'd cast from the rocks, often a futile gesture since fish rarely fed close to shore.

One windy, choppy evening Bill Schaadt and I were in our boat at the third light.

"Look." Bill pointed.

On the bridge, hunched against the railing, oblivious to speeding traffic and thoroughly unable to distinguish Bill or me, was Walt clutching an enormous spinning rod. Cocking it back, he used it to drive his lure in a trajectory which carried it over a school of bass I'm sure he never saw. His face was locked in an expression of determination that did not make him look any less like an angling Ichabod Crane.

"Boy," Bill said, "now there's a guy who likes to fish!" As we'd hoped and anticipated, Walt hooked a striper, stalked grimly back to the rocks, and landed it.

Several years passed during which I did not see Walt Mullen. Then one cold spring morning I was out at the bridge alone. To avoid the noisome mob of trollers, with whom the bridge had become a favorite haunt, I'd begun going at odd hours and poorish tides. When it grew light I saw a figure on the rocks, casting. Walt! I drew up my anchor and rowed in, circling widely so I wouldn't spoil anything. Close in, I turned but could no longer see anyone.

I went ashore and called out, but got no response. I looked under the bridge and finally crossed the freeway to search the other side. There was no one. I felt a deep sense of loss, an uneasy melancholy. I went home.

Later I found out Walt had died earlier that spring.

*A mystical morning unfolds around a fly fisherman on Oregon's Gold Lake. (Photograph © Dennis Frates)*

I row around behind Frank. The bass are there and I see the heavy swirls as they feed. Traffic on the bridge is picking up, early commuters. They are too low in their cars to see us but the truck drivers give a wave or short blast of the horn. It is getting light, a gray dawn that I imagine could be heavily depressing to a man facing eight hours on the production line.

"The coldest winter I ever spent," wrote someone, "was a summer in San Francisco." I wonder momentarily if this, in part, explains the high suicide rate and high alcohol intake for which the City on the Bay is known. Frank and I are virtually within sight of well over a million people, yet alone. We are perhaps out of step, ill-placed and ill-timed, in a sphere where cogs must mesh and all parts syncopate to keep the system running smoothly. Even within the framework of angling as a popular endeavor, our methods are archaic: fly-rods and rowboats. But we are touching something unrestricted, wild and arcane, beyond the reach of those who carefully maintain one-dimensional lives. I know there are people in the city nearby whose one contact today with unreconstructed nature will be to step in a diminutive pile of poodle excrement.

When I looked into the mirror during the late fifties I saw a striped-bass fisherman who often imagined, wrongly, that he was doing something remarkable and unique.

At the time an old gent by the name of Ellis Springer was pier keeper for the Marin Rod and Gun Club, which was situated only a few feet from the bridge. He let me use the club's launching ramp, dock, and fish-cleaning table even though I was not a member.

Ellis was never seen without a light-blue captain's hat and stubby cigar. He talked often of the days he'd spent in the Spanish-American War but his manner of speech was so unique that you could understand nothing of what he said. I didn't think he knew what fly-fishing was, and wanting to let him in on my little discovery, I gave a demonstration one day off the dock. He looked properly astonished and when I showed him my flies, he became incoherently excited, exclaiming, "Yeeehhh! Hoopty poopty! Hoopty poopty!"

These exclamations became a permanent part of all subsequent conversations.

"Hi, Springer."

"Eeeeehhh! Hoopty poopty!"

I used to carry fish around in the back of my car the way other kids my age carried a six-pack of Country Club. I'd show Ellis and he'd become truly frantic.

"Yeeeehhh! Hoopty poopty! Hoopty poopty!"

Gradually I became aware of the fact he called everything that was not strictly a sardine fillet a hoopty poopty.

Frank hooks a bass. I put my anchor down out of his way but still close enough to reach the school. I see two powerful boils and cast the bulky fly on a slow loop toward the swirl closest to a piling. I overshoot so the fly tinks against the bridge, hanging momentarily between the rail and roadway. As it flutters downward I see the number 9 stenciled above on an abutment.

The take is authoritative and my response lifts the clearly visible fly line from the water, curving it abruptly to the left as a sheet of droplets limns the fish's first long run. It is not a frenetic contest as the striper stays deep, far from the boat. But I am not inclined to carry out these contests gently and soon have the fish nearby. Once, glowering, he shoots away beneath a crescent of spray only to be turned in a vertical wallow. After all, nothing in their lives really prepares fish to deal with the relentless ordeal of being hooked. Walt Mullen described playing a fish by saying, "then it fooled around and fooled around." And that is exactly it.

In the boat the fish is big.

"It's more than twenty-five," I say to Frank.

Earlier we had discussed a twenty-five-pound striper caught accidentally by a fly-fisherman in the Russian River. It seemed more appropriate that a fish taken by design should receive top honors for the season. Naturally, we both expressed the hope that one of us would catch such a fish. Now, back at the beach, we lay three large bass in front of the *Cable Crossing* sign.

"That one's bigger than the thirty-pounder I caught last season," says Frank. He takes a Polaroid of me holding the fish, and a minute later the image appears, looking distant and journalistic. After I promise to call him as soon as I get the thing weighed, I head for San Rafael and Frank goes off to work in San Francisco.

*A brilliant summer day lures two dry fly fishermen to California's famed Fall River. (Photograph © R. Valentine Atkinson)*

Later, I call.

"It's big, isn't it?" Frank asks right away. "I've been looking at this snapshot all morning.

"Yes. Thirty-six pounds, six ounces."

The record Joe Brooks had held for eighteen years was broken. When I got to know Joe he would always introduce me as "a great salt-water fisherman," which was embarrassing because while he was alive he was so clearly the greatest. Now others have caught bigger bass, eliminating my personal stake in the matter. It is a relief to be reminded that competition in angling is entirely beside the point and that I'm simply an angler of average persuasion and ability who happened to cast a fly near a large, hungry fish one morning. Besides, there are too many other things to think about, like a certain broad shovel on the porch. I finished all the Jack Daniels last night and this morning I am hopelessly snowed in.

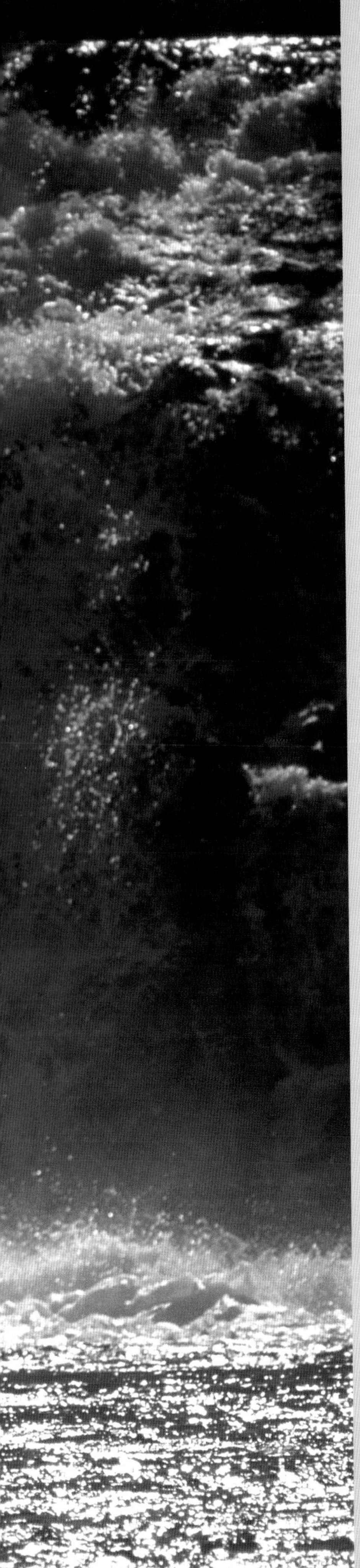

Chapter Six

# In Defense of Fly Fishing

"One thing is abundantly clear—fly fishing is supercharged with mysterious, magnetic stuff."

*—A. J. McClane, "Drops Those Daggers, Man!"*

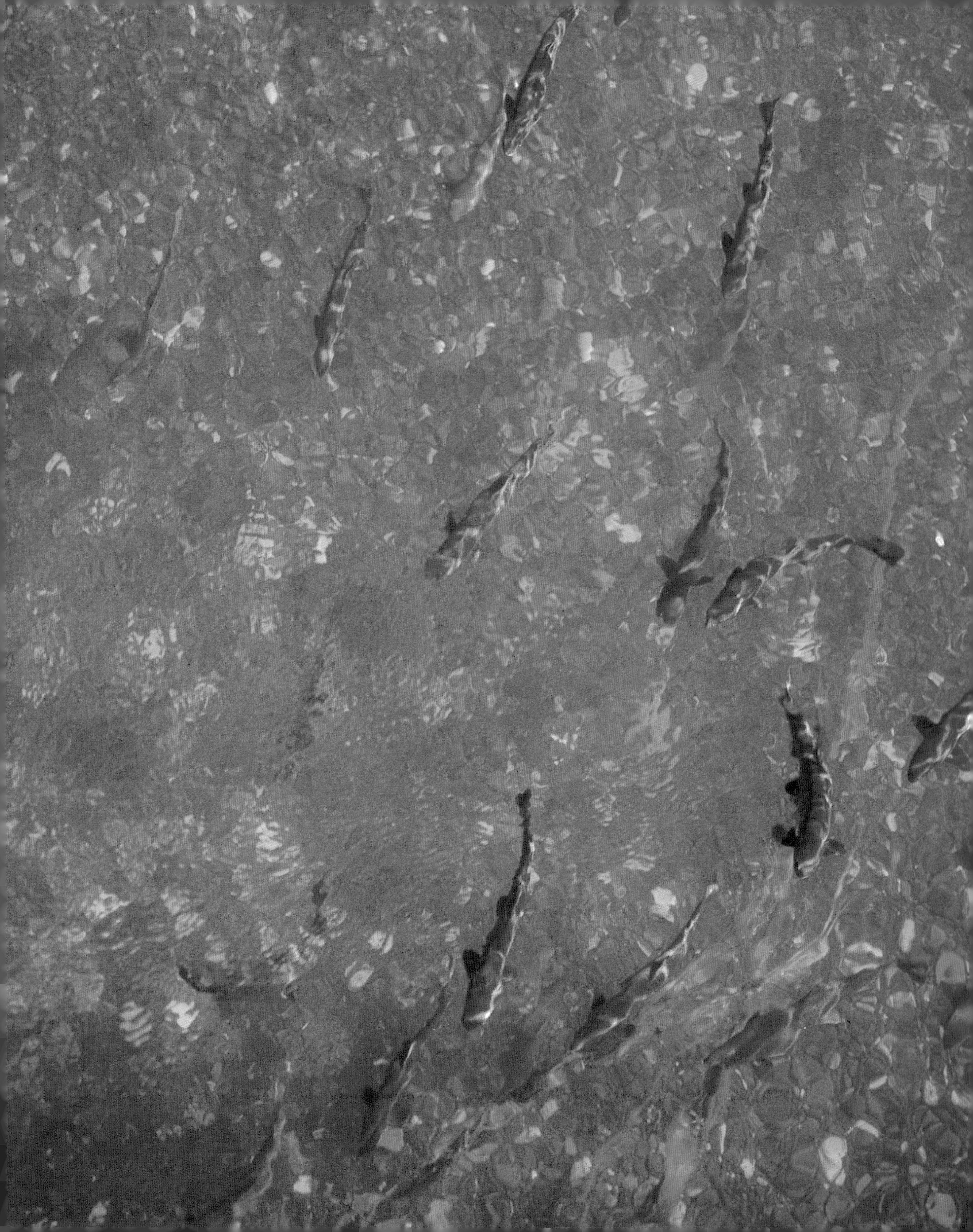

# The Point of View

By George La Branche

George Michel Lucien La Branche (1875-1961) was the ultimate dry fly man. His classic of fly fishing literature, *The Dry Fly and Fast Water* (1914), established La Branche as the father of American-style dry fly fishing. Breaking away from British methods, La Branche emphasized reading water and fly presentation, concepts that endure to this day.

In 1906, La Branche helped form the Angler's Club of New York, an American version of the Fly Fisher's Club in London. In addition, La Branche leaves a rich fly-tying legacy. He is credited with the invention of the Pink Lady, a spin-off of the King of the Waters, and his tied flies are exhibited in the American Museum of Fly Fishing.

This chapter from *The Dry Fly and Fast Water* illustrates, with passionate clarity, La Branche's conviction that dry fly fishing is the highest art of angling.

PREVIOUS PAGE, MAIN IMAGE: *Lewis Falls, named for Captain Meriwether Lewis, crashes beyond a fly fishermen in Yellowstone National Park. (Photograph © Jeff Henry/Roche Jaune Pictures, Inc.)*

PREVIOUS PAGE, INSET IMAGE: *Dating from the 1890s, this photograph features two stoic fishermen and an afternoon's catch from the Rattlesnake River. (Courtesy of the Montana Historical Society, Helena)*

LEFT: *A school of cutthroat trout gather in gemlike waters. (Photograph © Jeff Henry/Roche Jaune Pictures, Inc.)*

*Anglers release a fly-caught cutthroat into the Snake River. (Photograph © R. Valentine Atkinson)*

THE CAPTURE OF a splendid ouananiche under circumstances most trying is somewhere described by a well-known writer, who, in his inimitable style, exhibits himself before his readers running through his entire assortment of artificial flies, first one and then another and still another, and all without avail. We see him casting, casting, all impatience, determined, perhaps exasperated. Surely some sort of lure is predicated. But what? Ah, he has it! A live grasshopper. Then follows the pursuit, the overtaking, and the capture of the grasshopper, the impaling of its unfortunate body, its proffer to the fish, a desperate battle, and, finally, the contemplation of the finest fish of the season safely landed. The thrilling moment! Which was it? Why, of all moments, that one in which he captured the grasshopper! The story affords a fine illustration of what I call the "point of view," but until after the revelation that came to me with my first success with the dry fly, I did not fully appreciate its finer and deeper meanings.

A certain pleasurable excitement always attends the taking of a good fish by the true angler. Yet, after all, the quality of his gratification should be measured by the method of capture. In angling, as in all other arts, one's taste and discrimination develop in proportion to his opportunity to see, study, and admire the work of greater artists. Even as a knowledge of the better forms of music leads, eventually, to a distaste for the poorer sorts, and as familiarity with the work of great painters leads to disgust with the chromo-lithograph-like productions of the dauber, so, too, does a knowledge of the higher and more refined sorts of angling lead just as surely to the ultimate abandonment of the grosser methods. One who has learned to cast the fly seldom if ever returns to the days when he was content to sit upon the bank, or the string-piece of a pier, dangling his legs overboard while he watched his cork bobbing up and down, indicating by its motions what might be happening to the bunch of worms at the hook end of the line; and, even as casting the fly leads to the abandonment of the use of bait, so, too, does the dry fly lead to the abandonment of the wet or sunk fly. There can be no question but that the stalking of a rising trout bears to the sport of angling the same relation to its grosser forms as the execution of a symphony bears to the blaring of the local brass band. It appeals to the higher and more aesthetic qualities of the mind, and dignifies the pot-hunter's business into an art of the highest and finest character.

I am thus brought to the consideration of the pot-hunter and the fish hog. Many angling writers there be who have not hesitated, nor have they been ashamed, to describe the taking of great numbers of trout on separate and many occasions. They feel, no doubt, that such narratives entitle them to consideration as authorities on the subject. I quote from one—who shall be nameless—his bragging description of a perfect slaughter of fish. After telling of twenty-five or thirty trout taken during midday, naming at least a dozen flies he had found *killing*, he concludes: "All my trout were taken from the hook and *thrown twenty-five* feet to shore. Thirty, my friend claimed, yet when I came to count tails I found *forty* as handsome trout as ever man wished to see, and all caught from six in the evening until dark, about seven forty-five. I had no net or creel, therefore had to lead my trout into my hand. The friend at whose house I was staying claims I lost more than I caught by having them flounder off the hook *while trying to take them by the gills and by flinging them ashore*." The italics are mine. And this fellow had the temerity to add that some poor devil (an itinerant parson, he called him) annoyed him by wading in and fishing with a "stick cut from the forest." Had Washington Irving witnessed this fellow's fishing I doubt that he would have been moved to write: "There is certainly something in angling that tends to produce a gentleness of spirit and a pure serenity of mind."

There are men calling themselves anglers—save the mark!—who limit the number of fish to the capacity of creel and pockets, and to whom size means merely compliance with the law—a wicked law, at that, which permits the taking of immature trout. It is not an inspiring sight to see a valiant angler doing battle with a six-inch trout, and, after brutally subjecting it to capture, carefully measuring it on the butt of his rod which he has marked for the purpose, stretching it, if necessary, to meet the law's requirements, and in some cases, if it does not come up to the legal standard, rudely flinging it away in disgust—to die as a result of its mishandling. Happily, this tribe is not increasing, because of the persistent efforts of true sportsmen who do not hesitate to denounce it publicly whenever opportunity arises. Perhaps it is permissible to hope that the pot-hunter and the fish hog may in time disappear, but, if this desirable end is to be brought about, true sportsmen must not shun their duty but must wage unceasing war against them.

Books on angling abound in word-pictures descriptive of the strenuous battle of the hooked fish to escape its captor, many such pictures being so vividly drawn that the reader fairly imagines himself in the writer's waders, his excitement ending only when the captive is in the net. It is meet, therefore, that some consideration be given to the point of view of those anglers who believe that great merit attaches to him who lands a good fish on light tackle.

There can be no question of the excitement attending the playing of a good trout nor of the skill required in its handling, and this excitement, in proportion to the ideas of the individual, is a greater or less measure of the sport; but, given the opportunity, it is my opinion that, in the hands of a skilful angler, the rod will kill nine out of ten fish hooked. Be that as it may, can the degree of skill, even with the lightest tackle, displayed in the landing of a two or three pound trout (a fine fish on our Eastern streams) bear comparison with that required in the capture of a

*Anglers trade secrets on Montana's Gallatin River. (Photograph © R. Valentine Atkinson)*

six-foot tarpon on a six-ounce rod and a six-strand line? A six-foot tarpon will weigh about one hundred and twenty pounds, and the line will bear a deadweight strain of twelve pounds. Compare this with the three-pound trout taken on a gut leader, the weakest link in the angler's chain, which will lift a weight of two or more pounds, and the futility of beguiling oneself with the belief that the trout has any advantage will be apparent.

The playing of a trout is undeniably part of the sport, but, however difficult one wishes to make it, it is but secondary to the pleasure derived from casting the fly and deluding that old trout into mistaking it for a bit of living food. It is this art, this skill, this study of the fish itself and its habits, that places dry fly fishing for trout far ahead of all other forms of angling. It has been said that there is no sport that requires in its pursuit a greater knowledge of the game, more skill, more perseverance, than fly fishing, and that no sport holds its votaries longer. I am quite of this opinion. "There is no genuine enjoyment in the easy achievement of any purpose," and in fly fishing a full measure of satisfaction is obtained only when the taking of a single fish is accomplished under conditions most difficult and trying.

*A rainbow tricked by a dry fly surges against the line. (Photograph © Doug Stamm)*

The true angler is content only when he feels that he has taken his fish by the employment of unusual skill. The highest development of this skill at the present state of the angler's art is the dry fly method. I do not deny that there are many anglers who have carried sunk fly and even worm casting to a high degree of specialisation and refinement; yet it seems to me—nay, more than that, it is a positive conviction with me—that no manner of sunk fly or worm or bait casting bears any sort of favourable comparison to the dry fly. I know that in this country, at least, the dry fly man is accused by his sunk fly fellows of being affected, dogmatic, fanatic. Yet it is not so. The dry fly man has passed through all of the stages of the angler's life, from the cane pole and the drop-line to the split bamboo and the fur-and-feather counterfeit of the midge fly. He has experienced throes of delight each time he advanced from the lower to the higher grade of angler. I insist that I do not make my words too strong when I say that in all of angling there is no greater delight than that which comes to the dry fly angler who simulates a hatch of flies, and entices to the surface of the water a fish lying hidden, unseen, in the stronghold of his own selection. Let him who doubts put aside his prejudice long enough to give the premier method fair trial, and soon he will be found applying for the highest degree of the cult—"dry fly man."

# Fishing Jewelry

By Sigurd F. Olson

Conservationist Sigurd Ferdinand Olson (1899-1982) was the North Country's greatest champion. He canoed its lakes and streams, wrote with eloquence of its beauty and solitude, and guided others through its magnificent wilderness.

In 1922, one of the travelers he guided was Will Dilg, president of a fledgling organization formed to protect fishing streams: the Izaak Walton League of America. Olson guided Dilg through lake country damaged by unchecked logging; in turn, Dilg promised the league's commitment to this threatened wilderness. The northern wilderness they fought to preserve is now treasured as the peerless Boundary Waters Canoe Area Wilderness.

Olson's books include *The Singing Wilderness* (1956), *Listening Point* (1958), *The Lonely Land* (1961), and *Reflections from the North County* (1976). His essays continue to serve as a hallmark of nature writing.

The following article first appeared in 1925 in the Milwaukee *Journal*. In it, an old-timer's tip sends Olson fly fishing for black bass on a pristine northern lake.

LEFT: *"Let me hear the soft pop and burble of my deerhair bug and the heart-stopping glug of a largemouth inhaling it."–William G. Tapply, A Fly-Fishing Life, 1997 (Photograph © Doug Stamm)*

THE TWO OF US, "Wild Cat" Dan and I had just stowed away enough fish mulligan to last us a week and were enduring the ominous silence that always comes between such an achievement and the inevitable suggestion, "Well guess we'd better clean up the mess."

After some fifteen minutes of bliss, I looked at Dan and he at me, both with the same blank expression of helplessness. Finally Dan heaved a ponderous sigh and rose to his feet. "Well," he started in, "I suppose," and he looked at me rather pleadingly, "I guess partner, I've et too much. Let's leave the dishes tills mornin'."

"Good idea Dan," answered I, greatly relieved. "Guess we both feel the same way."

With one accord, we pushed the supper dishes to the end of the table, just far enough back in the dark, so that they couldn't reproach us visibly at least for not washing them. It was all we could do after that, to stagger over to our respective bunks. Our pipes were soon going and a feeling of lazy comfort and peace pervaded the cabin.

As I watched the blue smoke curl up around the rafters, I wouldn't have traded places then with anyone else in the world. I knew then as I have often known since, that there is nothing so soul-satisfying and conducive to perfect contentment, as a full stomach and a good place to rest, after a day in the brush. Then to top it off, the rain began to patter softly against the south windows. The hour was ripe for dreams.

*A hungry largemouth bass bursts from the lily pads in this watercolor by Minnesota artist and photographer Bob White.*

Neither of us said a word for perhaps a half an hour. From my corner, I could see old Dan sitting on the edge of his bunk, eyes half closed, smoking contentedly. Presently he started taking short spasmodic puffs and I waited expectantly. A few long puffs and he began, "You was askin' me t'other day 'bout bass, and since then I've been thinkin' 'bout a fellow that came up here some eight or nine years ago. He was plumb crazy 'bout fishin', and had the dangdest outfit along, you ever did see, little red flies, white ones, brown ones, and all sorts of funny wooden bugs. When I saw it the first time, I asked him what he planned on doin' with all that pile o' jewelry. He laffed and said, he was goin' to show us lumber jacks how to ketch bass. Well, I'd caught plenty of 'em with frogs and minners and told him so, but never in all my life with such an ornery collection as what he had. Between you and me, I thought he was a little bit off, but told him to go ahead an' see what he could do.

"Then he started askin' me where they was any, and I told him we used to ketch 'em pretty plenty up at Grass Lake, some twenty years ago, when this camp was runnin' logs down the river, but that it hadn't been fished much since.

"Right away this feller gets interested and wants to know where it was. I told him as clost as I could figger, it was 'bout a mile northwest of Bray Lake, an' as far as I knew there wan'n't no trail. Just the same he was bound to go and stayed with me all that night.

"Well, next mornin' before daylight, he was hittin' the brush an' he didn't come back till just before dark, but dang it all if he didn't have the fines' string o' bass I ever did see. Right then and there, I took back all I'd said about his jewelry. Before he left he gave me a couple o' those bugs an' flies, but I never did get time to try 'em out. One o'those bass he brought in must a'weighed seven pounds if he weighed an ounce."

Then followed a long series of puffs.

"Son," he said after some time, "I'd like to see you go up an' try that lake. They must be some big ones in there yet. In the ole days we had a scow up there an' in the early mornin's, jus' when the mist was risin' off o' the rushes round the aidge, we'd ketch all we could eat with a couple o' frogs before breakfast.

By that time, I was sitting bolt upright on the edge of my bunk, wondering if I was really awake. Imagine having an old timer tell you of a lake that had hardly been fished for twenty years and full of bass up to seven pounds or more. Before I had time to ask him about the location of the lake Dan told me where I'd find a stub of a pencil and an old envelope.

"I'm pretty old and stiff to go up myself but I can tell you pretty close how to get there," he assured me. "Now if you'll gimme your pencil I'll try and draw you a map."

Slowly and laboriously he sketched a rough map on the back of the envelope, then with the stem of his pipe he traced the trail from Bray to Grass Lake.

"Foller up the shore of Bray Lake north from the cabin till you strike a swale, then strike straight northwest for three-quarters of a mile and there you'll find her right in front of you. You can' miss it."

I stowed the map away religiously in my shirt pocket. "That's news to me, Dan," I answered, "and if I don't bring back the brother to that seven pounder tomorrow night, I'll buy you grub for a month."

We smoked awhile longer and talked bass, deer hunting, and game laws, till we were both sleepy and then turned in. I was far too excited to think of sleep, but finally dropped off only to dream of monster black bass striking insanely at every cast. Right in the midst of it, I was awakened by Dan's, "Roll out. Daylight in the swamp."

Breakfast was finished hurriedly, and I plunged into the rain-drenched brush just as daylight was breaking over the east shore of Bray Lake. I might just as well have taken an ice cold shower, for in a minute I was soaked to the skin. I followed

*A lovely brace of fly-caught crappies. (Photograph © Doug Stamm)*

*"Bass–A Critical Moment"–this image was created circa 1910 by American artist Oliver Kemp (1887-1934), whose illustrations often graced the covers of magazines such as the Saturday Evening Post.*

Dan's map carefully and in half an hour found myself on a high brushy hill overlooking a tiny alder-fringed lake, not half a mile away. Then followed a mad scramble through some of the densest jumble I had ever seen. The entire slope was burned over and grown up thickly with popple brush and the ground itself, a maze of charred windfalls interlaced with the prickly vines of raspberry. Half the time, I was balanced precariously on downed timber or extricating myself from a network of tangled brush.

Arriving finally at the lake, I found the shore was partly sand and partly mud. All along the edge lay windfalls with inviting bunches of lily pads nestling around their submerged tips. I hit the shore at just such a spot and nervously rigged up my tackle.

While trying to fasten a brown fly to a swivel spinner, I succeeded in running the hook clean through the arm of my shirt. I tried most carefully to back it out, but try as I might, the barb refused to come. It seemed as though I had worked half the morning, before I finally ripped it out in sheer desperation.

Wading out to my waist, so that I could cast without encumbering myself with the whole shoreline, I unlimbered and let the fly sail out toward a bunch of lily pads. It settled gracefully on the edge of a leaf, rested just a second and slipped off. Bang! and a big green form splashed the whole end of the windfall. I let him have it and struck. Yes, I struck and my bedraggled fly came dancing merrily back over the disturbed ripples. I cast again and again, but not another rise did I get. Finally deciding that I must have hooked him pretty badly, I left the windfall and waded up the shore, casting at every likely spot. Some places literally screamed black bass, but no lure I had would bring even a half-hearted strike. By ten o'clock I had fished clear around the lake with only one strike to my record and that the first. I was pretty discouraged and was beginning to think that Old Dan's story was a fizzle or that I was a no good excuse for a fisherman.

I sat down on a log to think things over, wondering if there wasn't some place I had missed. I did remember one, where the mud had been so soft that I couldn't wade out to east, and had gone back through the alders to the next likely spot. It was halfway around the lake, but nevertheless I decided to try it, so back I went, creeping carefully through the brush until I was at the water's edge. The mud was much too soft to hold me, so I stepped on a log lying near, without touching the windfall at whose end I was to cast. It was rather a ticklish place at best, for the brush grew so close to the shore that casting was difficult.

Finding a little opening in the leaves, I tipped my rod back and sailed the fly out over the end of the windfall. It lit gently a few inches from a big lily pad at its very tip. Slap! A boiling swirl of water and the fly started for depths unknown. This time I hooked him firmly and the fight was on. First he dashed for a tangle of half-sunken brush, then just as wildly for the lily pads further out. At every run, I expected to see the line come floating limply to the top. Then down he went and by the fierce, tugging jerks I knew that he was sulking at the bottom. Keeping my balance on the slippery log made it doubly interesting. Once, as I lost my balance, I stepped in up to my knees in the soft ooze and let out ten feet of precious slack while getting back on.

I thought that was the finish but when I recovered my line, he was still on. Finally he seemed to be tiring, so I began to urge him a little, but no sooner did he feel the added pressure, than out he sped again for deep water. Out, out, he went, while the handle whizzed through my fingers. I tried to hold him back, but still the reel screeched. Only a few yards left, when all of a sudden he stopped dead and started to sulk. Here I got in a few yards of slack and thinking he was done for, began to bring him in. This time he changed his tactics. In he rushed straight toward me, while I reeled madly. When about twenty feet away, out of the water he came shaking his head in a last desperate effort. Not once, but three times did he come, making each jump wilder than the one before. All I could do was wind, wind, and keep the tip of my rod down.

*An angler lands a smallmouth bass in this 1904 painting by American artist Henry Sumner Watson (1868-1933). Watson, who worked as an illustrator for Scribner's magazine, specialized in outdoors art.*

The third jump took his last ounce of strength, for after that he came in sullenly. I slipped my hands into his gills and lifted from the water one of the finest bass it has ever been my joy to catch, and one of the best fighters. I laid him down tenderly on a bed of moss and for a long time watched the play of light on the bronze and green of his scales. It was one of those supreme moments that come in the life of every fisherman when he realizes for once, that the big one didn't get away.

After that Grass Lake seemed more cheerful. The sky was bluer and the birds sang more light heartedly than ever. I had solved the mystery and every windfall after that, was cast at not from the water, but from the shore. By late afternoon I had landed two more splendid fish, almost as large as the first and not a one under five pounds.

If I had used a boat, I would have had my limit, but I was more than satisfied. I had discovered a new sport, one as yet unrivaled for me, stalking black bass from the shore. It was almost dark before I reached the cabin at Bray Lake. As I came down the trail Old Dan saw me and yelled, "What luck?"

I answered as unconcernedly as I could, "Oh, I got a few Dan." It seemed as though I never would reach the cabin after that, even though it was only a scant hundred yards away. I did finally arrive however, and with great inward satisfaction spread out my catch for his appraisal.

For a moment he looked at them in silence. "Well I'll be danged," was all he said. "If that fool jewelry ain't turned the trick again."

# *Blood Knots*

*By Mallery Burton*

Mallory Burton makes her home in Prince Rupert, where she fly fishes for salmon and steelhead and works as a linguist and teacher for Special Education Technology-British Columbia.

Burton's essays and short fiction regularly appear in angling magazines such as *Fly Rod & Reel* and *Fly Fishing*. Her work has been collected into two books, *Reading the Water: Stories and Essays of Flyfishing and Life* (1995) and *Green River Virgins: And Other Passionate Anglers* (2000). Burton, as one critic writes, "knows more than fish and streams and tackle; she knows the hearts and minds of the humans who are happiest when they are waist-deep in a wild river."

Burton's prose returns again and again to the woman fly fisher—explored here with intimate clarity and emotion. This story was first published in the Winter 1990 issue of *Flyfisher* magazine and later anthologized in *A Different Angle: Fly Fishing Stories by Women* (1996).

LEFT: *An angler fishing the Yellowstone River upstream from Nez Perce Ford is rewarded by a cutthroat trout. (Photograph © Jeff Henry/Roche Jaune Pictures, Inc.)*

I HAVE NEGLECTED to tie the wading boots properly, to pull the braided laces tight against the metal grommets, to fasten them securely with a double knot. This is partly due to lack of effort and partly because the boots are much too big for me. They belong to my father. Belonged to my father. I suppose they are mine now. Neither my mother nor my sister fishes. I am the only one.

The boots are full of fine gravel, which chafes between my thick, outer wading socks and the lightweight fabric of these summer waders. I should get out of the river to empty the boots, but it doesn't seem worth the effort of battling the current all the way back to the bank.

A mosquito buzzes close to my temple. I can hear its thin whine over the rushing of the steam, see the dark fluttering blur out of the corner of my eye. The insect lands, and I feel its sting, such a tiny prick that I wonder why I have always made such a fuss about them, slapping at myself and smearing poisonous oil all over my face and limbs.

I slowly raise my hand to my temple and crush the mosquito. Not because I really want to, but because I feel I should. The same way that I felt I should wash my face and comb my hair and put on my clothes this morning, even though it seemed to make such little sense. It is unsettling, this doubting of routine, this absence of concern, this lack of energy. Perhaps I should not be here on the river at all.

"Go. Get out of the house for a while," my mother insisted. She extended her arms and flicked her hands at me as though I were a bothersome child. "There's really nothing you can do until this afternoon."

My father died two days ago. The funeral is today at four. Mother is handling it pretty well. My sister is distraught, sedated. I am still waiting for my own emotion to surface in what I anticipate will be a sense of overwhelming loss. Every few hours, I test the depth of my grief, sounding its progress with tentative excursions into the past.

Earlier this morning, I sorted through my father's fly fishing gear. I have gear of my own, of course, but it isn't something you think of packing when your father has died suddenly and you are trying to catch a plane at an impossible hour. I sorted his flies and mended his leaders. I removed the spool from his old Hardy reel to change it over from a right-handed to a left-handed retrieve. I had to unwind all the line in order to rewind it onto the spool in the opposite direction.

The gear was spread out all over the kitchen floor. A neighbor woman, who'd come by with a tray of baking for after the service, had to pick her way through the mess. Seeing the tangle of line on the floor, she offered to help. She held the line with a slight tension so that I could wind it more evenly onto the spool. She kept looking at the split-cane rod lying in sections near her feet. My father's name had been burned into the shaft in an old-fashioned, flowing script.

"This is beautiful old gear," she said. "Are you going fishing?"

"Yes."

"You're not," said my mother. She shut off the running water and turned, twisting her hands in her apron.

*Worn from multiple readings, a favorite fly fishing book rests against an assortment of beautiful gear, including Nottingham fly reels. (Photograph © Howard Lambert)*

"You said get out of the house."

"I thought maybe a walk." She shrugged and left the room. I expected the neighbor woman to follow her, instead, she motioned me to continue my winding.

"Do you think it's strange, going fishing? At a time like this, I mean?"

The woman hesitated. Then she leaned forward and said, very quietly, "Sometimes it takes a while to catch up with you. When Alex passed away, I didn't even cry. A couple of weeks later I was coming through the door with my arms full of groceries, and the wind caught the door, slammed it shut behind me. I put down the groceries, opened the door and slammed it again. I must have slammed it twenty times."

I pictured the slight gray-haired woman slamming the door, understanding her satisfaction with the final, solid sound of it. The hatch is beginning. At first there is just a handful of bugs coming off the water, teasing a few eager fish into splashy rises. The nearest fisherman is a hundred yards upstream, stationed in one spot, not casting. Presumably he is waiting for the better fish to show themselves. He looks alert, expectant as the swarm of swallows gathering overhead.

I know this river. The hatch will gradually accelerate over the next hours or so, until the smooth surface of the water is frothed and silver with feeding fish. Until the air is both noisy with lunging rises and soft with clouds of pale-winged mayflies.

The upstream fisherman has his rod in the air now, stripping line with his left hand while the length of his backcast grows. I have picked out my fish as well, a trout that shows the curved half-circle of his back with each leisurely rise. The fish is directly across from me.

I drop a delicate Pale Morning a few feet upstream, floating it dead-drift over his lie. I am in the right place, with just enough slack in my line to ensure a drag-free float, but my timing is off. The bugs are hatching in greater numbers now, and it is difficult to focus on the rhythm of my trout with fish rising sporadically on every side.

One larger fish, in particular, is coming up just a rod length away. His appearance is erratic, and his unexpected rises have twice startled me into lifting the tip of my rod, a reaction that makes the fly take a sudden skip over the water. Afraid that I will spook my fish, I decide to deliberately put down the erratic riser. I face

*A salmon fishing trip to Nuyakuk Falls, Alaska, inspired Bob White to paint this evocative scene, entitled "One-Cast Annie."*

upstream, waiting for the fish to surface again, quickly stripping in my line until most of it lies in a tangle, bunched against my waist by the current. A cloud passes over the sun momentarily, and the water goes steel-gray. When the fish shows, I slap the line down hard on the water's surface just behind his head. The fish snaps up the natural that was his target, then lunges sideways, seizing my imitation and taking it down with him.

*"A river is water in its loveliest form; rivers have life and sound and movement and infinity of variation, rivers are veins of the earth through which the life blood returns to the heart."—Roderick L. Haig-Brown, A River Never Sleeps, 1944 (Photograph © Jeff Henry/Roche Jaune Pictures, Inc.)*

For a few seconds the leader disappears, its surface coils pulled straight down by the fish. Then, with a great sucking splash, the trout suddenly shoots through the air. He is coming fast; straight at me, eye level. His mouth is open, and I can see the fly lodged securely in his upper jaw. His gills are flared open. Looking into his mouth and out through his gills, I can see the trees on the far shore. The fish is wide-eyed, and I wonder if he has seen me. He drops just short of hitting my chest, clumsily on his side, throwing water in my face.

The fish changes direction, runs upstream. The current does not appear to be much of a deterrent. The pile of line at my waist diminishes rapidly, and somehow I have the sense to let it go, to keep my hand off the reel. The last of the slack disappears, and the line slaps tight against the rod, sending out a shower of tiny droplets. For an instant I feel the weight of the fish connecting at the other end of the line in one strong pull, and then he is gone.

Damn. Damn. I want that fish. I lift the rod tip, aching for the fish to be there. I will play the fish carefully and bring him gently to the net. I will hold him in the current, admire his colors until he is strong enough to swim away on his own; instead, the line comes back easily through the water.

The fish will jump again, trying to shake the fly that is still hooked in his jaw. I will see the gleam of silver as his twisting body catches the sunlight. I stand looking upstream, but he does not show.

It is difficult to retrieve the line. My hands are shaking, and I feel weak, disoriented. The current tugs at my legs with a new intensity, as if the river has suddenly risen six inches. In turning, I lose my footing. My feet slide over the smooth stones and gravel bottom of the river, carried by the current. It occurs to me that if I fall, I will not have the strength to regain a footing. I concentrate on remaining upright, leaning into the current, angling slowly across the river toward shallower water and the protection of a small island. Slowly I make my way to the water's edge and sit down heavily on the bank, where I lie back in the rushes, my feet tailing in the water.

My father's death was sudden, unexpected. The secretary found him face down on his desk when she went in with the morning mail. It is difficult to believe. He was the sort of man you'd expect to perish on the side of a mountain heading for the continental divide. Or on the bank of an icy river during the winter steelhead run.

The sun is warm on my face. A mayfly, a survivor, crawls up on the underside of a reed and hangs upside down on its tip, swaying. There is a cold spot on my right instep where the gravel in my father's boot has finally punctured a small hole. It is just as well. If I get off the river now, I will just have time to drive back and change for the funeral.

I sit up and quickly untie the boots, keeping one eye on the river. I dump the gravel, rinse the boots, and retie the laces with a secure double knot. I repair the leader, adding lengths of fresh tippet with a series of secure blood knots. I carefully attach a new fly. The hatch could go on for hours. There are still plenty of fish rising. I wonder if my mother and sister will understand.

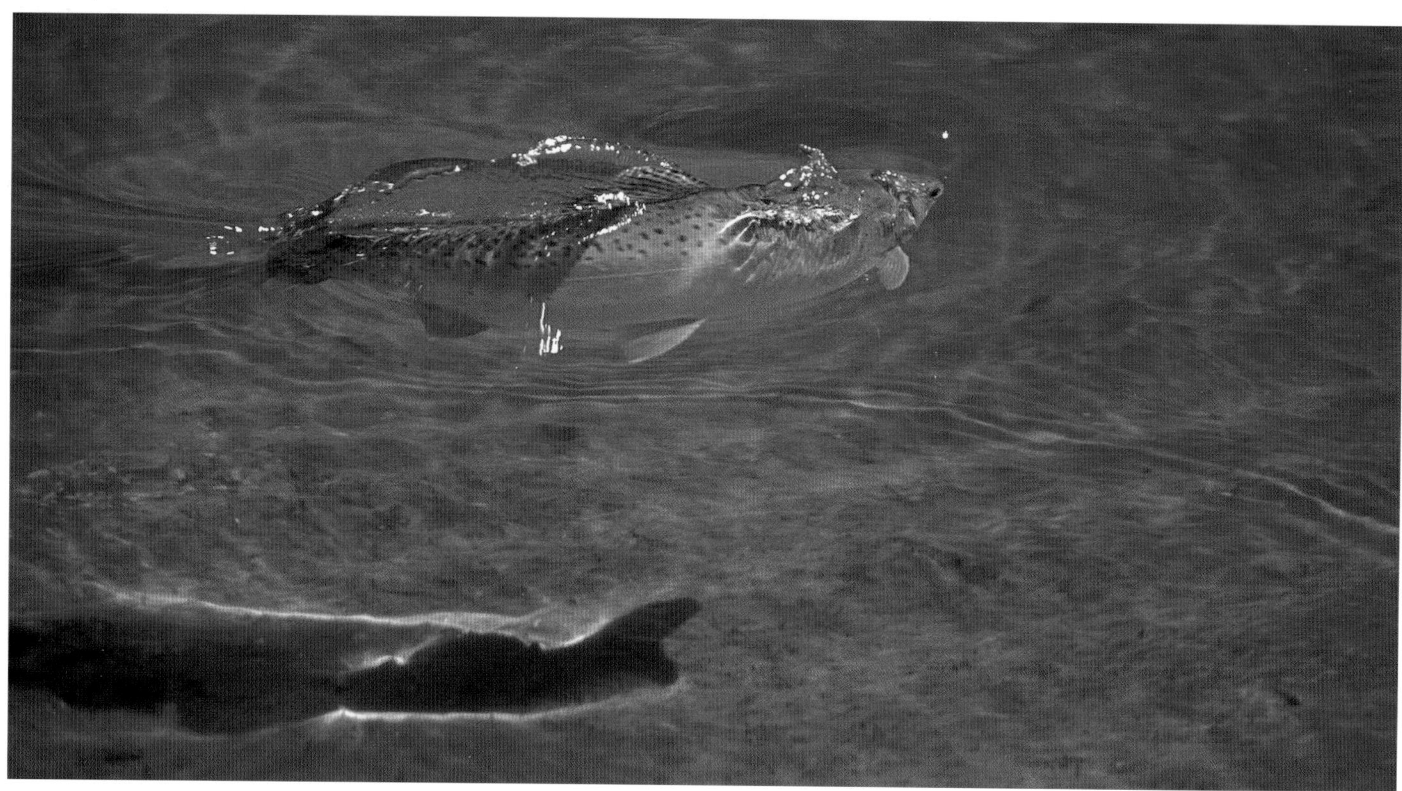

*A rainbow trout swirls the water's surface. (Photograph © Doug Stamm)*

# WIND KNOTS AND WET FEET

I'M A FLY-FISHERMAN. You've seen me in a long canoe fishing the Restigouche for Atlantic salmon. Or in a flat-bottomed skiff poled along the flats of Florida stalking bonefish. We've stood side by side in sleet on opening day on the Beaverkill—and in snow at the tag end of things on the Madison. We've argued steelhead flies on the Babine, brown trout methods on the Pere Marquette.

You've seen me popping for bass in Georgia and heard me bragging about wet-fly bream in Tennessee. And when they're running—be it shad or stripers—I'll do my best to be there. Unless I'm out for tarpon, or blues—or brookies.

I love those long, slender sticks and all the stuff that goes with them—waders and wet feet not excepted.

I've got four of everything except flies, where I do a little better than that. And reels and rods and matching lines, just in case. My vest weighs ten pounds, and I never have all the stuff along that I need. I'm an authority on high water, low water, bad tides, and wind knots.

I'm never convinced I've got the right fly—unless there's a fish attached—which is seldom. I know everything there is to know about landing fish—except when I get too excited to remember—which is always.

I can't double-haul, tie more than two knots, or recognize much more than a mayfly.

But I'm a fly-fisherman. I like the quiet company of pelicans, ospreys, wood ducks, and squirrels. I like the too-rare satisfaction of a perfect cast, the singsong of a running reel, and the etching of a fish against the sky. I like catching the same fish the second or third time more than catching him first. I like to hold him in my hand—then let him go.

But I don't catch much, to be honest—and I honestly don't care. I can be snagged, skunked, sunburned, or partially submerged—and still smile. If you don't think I'm crazy—you're a fly-fisherman too.

*—Gene Hill, Hill Country, 1978*

*An early morning angler is silhouetted against gleaming gray waters. (Photograph © Jeff Henry/Roche Jaune Pictures, Inc.)*

# Permissions

Voyageur Press has made every effort to determine original sources and locate copyright holders of the materials in this book. We gratefully acknowledge the writers, publishers, and agencies listed below for permission to reprint material copyrighted or controlled by them. Please bring to our attention any errors of fact, omission, or copyright.

"Fly Fishing Through the Midlife Crisis" by Howell Raines from *Fly Fishing Through the Midlife Crisis*. Copyright © 1993 by Howell Raines. Reprinted by permission of HarperCollins Publishers, Inc./William Morrow.

"A Quiet Week" by John Gierach from *Sex, Death, and Fly-fishing*. Copyright © 1990 by John Gierach. Reprinted by permission of Simon & Schuster Adult Publishing Group.

"Colorado Trails" by Zane Grey. Copyright © 1918 by Zane Grey. Reprinted by permission of Dr. Loren Grey and Zane Grey, Inc.

"Big Secret Trout" by Robert Travers from *Trout Madness*. Copyright © 1960 by John Voelker. Reprinted by permission of the John Voelker Foundation, the Voelker family, and Kitchie Hill, Inc.

"Backyard Trout" by Burton Spiller from *Fishin' Around*. Copyright © 1974 by Burton Spiller. Reprinted by permission of M. Ainslie Spiller.

"Potter's Fancy" by Corey Ford. Copyright © Corey Ford. Reprinted by permission of Dartmouth College Library.

"What Do You Do With All Your Spare Time?" by Louise Dickinson Rich from *We Took to the Woods*. Copyright © 1942 by Louise Dickinson Rich. Reprinted by permission of Dinah Rich Clark.

"Hooked" by Jan Zita Grover from *Northern Waters*. Copyright © 1999 by Jan Zita Grover. Reprinted by permission of Graywolf Press.

"In Pursuit of Bass" by Joan Salvato Wulff from *Joan Wulff's Fly Fishing*. Copyright © 1991 by Joan Salvato Wulff. Reprinted by permission of Stackpole Books.

"Upon the Earth Below" by Gordon MacQuarrie from *Stories of the Old Duck Hunters*. Copyright © 1967 by Gordon MacQuarrie. Reprinted by permission of Willow Creek Press, Inc.

"No Wind in the Willows" by Russell Chatham from *The Angler's Coast*. Copyright © 1976 by Russell Chatham. Originally published by Doubleday and Company; second edition © 1990 by Clark City Press. Reprinted by permission of Russell Chatham and Clark City Press.

"Blood Knots" by Mallory Burton. Copyright © 1990 by Mallory Burton. Reprinted by permission of Mallory Burton.